MONDRIAN
AND THE NEO-PLASTICIST UTOPIA

SERGE FAUCHEREAU

MONDRIAN
AND THE NEO-PLASTICIST UTOPIA

RIZZOLI
NEW YORK

First published in the United States of America in 1994 by

RIZZOLI INTERNATIONAL PUBLICATIONS, INC.
300 Park Avenue South, New York, NY 10010

© 1994 Ediciones Polígrafa, S. A.
Reproduction rights:
© 1994 ABC/Mondrian Estate/Holtzman Trust.
Licensed by International Licensing Partners B.V.
Text copyright © Serge Fauchereau
Translated by David Macey
Designed by Jordi Herrero

LC 94-66652
ISBN 0-8478-1832-2

Colour separations by
Teknocrom, S. A., L'Hospitalet de Llobregat (Barcelona)
Printed and bound by La Polígrafa, S. L.
Parets del Vallès (Barcelona)
Dep. Leg. B. 31.523 - 1994 (Printed in Spain)

CONTENTS

Self-portrait, 1912. Charcoal, 25 5/8 × 17 3/4 in. (65 × 45 cm). Gemeentemuseum, The Hague

The landscapes and general atmosphere of the Netherlands are not absolutely unique. The French province of Aunis, for example, which is the historical heartland of French Protestantism, is another flat region where the land merges imperceptibly into the sea. Cows graze in the marshlands around La Rochelle, and the flat countryside is fluted with canals dug long ago with the help of Dutch engineers, just as the shoreline and the islands are fluted with banks of earth marking the boundaries of the oyster beds and salterns. Further inland, the place names preserve traces of a maritime past; the villages have names like St. Pierre de l'Ile and Ile d'Albe, and Brouage, which is now far from the sea, was once a port.

Only a few verticals break the horizontality: lighthouses, towers, spires, and an occasional tall tree. History and technology have not succeeded in modifying this landscape to any great extent. I was born in Rochefort, which was built by Louis XIV to counter the Huguenots. The new city was laid out like a checkerboard on the edge of the marshes, but Louis XIV failed to see that long perfectly straight streets and perpendiculars punctuated with occasional rectangular squares were ideally suited to the very spirit he wanted to crush. I recall these features because they are the same in many parts of the world where men have had to struggle against the sea and the land, and because their struggles eventually create a *genius loci* that is difficult to resist. The Netherlands is merely an extreme example.

No matter which country they come from, trains slow down when they enter the Netherlands, not so much the towns are close together, as because the narrow track-bed does not allow the trains to travel at high speeds. Railway lines running between two canals cross a patchwork of fields separated by perfectly straight dikes; in springtime the tulips divide the fields that stretch as far as the eye can see into rectangles of red, yellow, and white — and the sky and the sea add blue. Most of the land has

been reclaimed from the sea, and was created by man in the course of a centuries-long struggle with nature. The geometry of the polders matches that of the tiles and the brick walls that Dutch artists loved so much. If we remove the human figure — and it is of secondary importance — from a painting by Pieter De Hooch (p. 8), all that remains is a perfect pattern of rectangles and squares. For his part, Pieter Saenredam (p. 8) is reluctant to paint human beings at all; they are tiny ants and can hardly be seen in his vast rectilinear and unadorned architectural structures. He is perhaps Piet Mondrian's most obvious ancestor. One is tempted to think of Baudelaire: "Here, everything is order and beauty, luxury, calm and voluptuousness." The order, the calm, and the beauty are real enough, but Baudelaire is a Latin. There is no luxury or voluptuousness in this Dutch world where comfort is readily sacrificed for the sake of aesthetics. That is why Gerrit Rietveld's famous chair, with its very rational lines and very clear colours, is so uncomfortable. But the chair is beautiful, very beautiful, or *schoon*, as they say in Dutch. *Schoon* simultaneously means beautiful, clean, and neat and tidy. When I lived on the corner of the Amstel and Van der Heijden Street, the word was constantly on the lips of the blonde lady whose house I shared. Nothing was beautiful or right if it was not where it should be. The pots and spotless mirrors all had their place within a definite order, and the furniture and the table legs were aligned with the straight lines of the parquet floor. And it was indeed beautiful and peaceful. As I made my way to the Stedelijk Museum, I ought to have taken this street and then that street, and when a lingering Latin perversity made me stray from my route, I discovered why when I encountered the cold wind blowing across a canal or down the wrong street. Yet my landlady, who was tolerant of foreigners and their ways, smiled understandingly. And everything was fine.

If we wish to understand the special

characteristics of the Dutch, we have to look at the enormous differences between Rembrandt's interiors or Vermeer's calm perspectives and the art of neighbouring countries, and compare them with the fleshy movement of Flemings like Rubens or Jordaens, and with the Germanic existential torments of Dürer or Cranach — and it is important to remember that Dürer and Cranach were neither Catholics nor Calvinists, but Lutherans. Having mentioned the climate of cultural tolerance, we also have to recall the possibility of a revolt against the levelheadedness of Vermeer and Mondrian; the outcome is the expressive turmoil of Van Gogh, who, like Mondrian, once thought of becoming a preacher. That is the other side of the same coin.

Anyone who wishes to understand Mondrian must, however, be wary of overly simplistic schemata. The painter obviously did not simply transpose the floral rectangles, the canals, and the play of horizontal and vertical lines of the Dutch landscape onto his neo-plasticist canvases. Yet there may be some basic geographic structure which is inscribed on the innermost depths of men, and which is echoed in their art. In recalling the stubborn struggle of a people against nature, or the Calvinist disapproval of "images," I am not suggesting that we find them reflected in the deliberation of Mondrian's art or in the aversion for figuration that he developed in his maturity. Yet an artist cannot escape certain archetypal structures of the mind, or the sensibility of his culture.

IN THE SERVICE OF ART

The life of Piet Mondrian is singularly lacking in the picturesque details that surround the lives of certain of the most popular artists. With the exception of the wars which forced him, like so many others, into exile, the few important events in his life were to a greater or lesser extent connected with art. The painter, whose real name was Piet Cornelis Mondriaan, was born in Amersfoot in 1872. His father was a militant Calvinist and a headmaster. It was his father who taught him the first rudiments of drawing. With the help of advice from his uncle Frits Mondriaan, a professional painter who enjoyed a favorable reputation, Piet qualified as an art teacher. After briefly being tempted by the idea of becoming a preacher, he finally turned to art

and worked unrelentingly to achieve his ambition. He enrolled as a student at the Rijks academie in Amsterdam, supported himself by making copies (fig. 1) and accepting various commissions, and exhibited with several art associations. In 1898 and 1901 he unsuccessfully entered the Prix de Rome competition. He travelled abroad on several occasions, but as in the case of his uncle and the Hague school (figs. 7–12), most of his inspiration came from the Dutch landscape. The Van Gogh retrospective at Amsterdam's Stedelijk Museum in 1905 brought him into contact with a more modern conception of painting. He was later impressed by the fauvist paintings of Kees van Dongen and was soon on good terms with Jan Sluyters and

Jan Toorop, who were amongst the most daring painters of the moment. He went to paint with Toorop in Domburg and in Westkapelle in Zeeland. Having adopted a broad divisionist style (figs. 26–28), he was, by 1908, one of Holland's most "advanced" painters, much to the dismay of his family and his uncle Frits, who criticised him severely. Mondrian was not, however, satisfied with his work. He adopted a clearer and more angular style of drawing, and at the same time became deeply absorbed in theosophical literature. The resulting plastic symbolism (figs. 32–36) did not satisfy him either. The works by the Parisian cubists that he saw at the Moderne Kunstring exhibition of 1911 had a profound impact on him and convinced him that he had to work in Paris. He went to Paris the following year, and lived in the same apartment block in Montparnasse as Lodewijk Schelfhout and Diego Rivera. After over two years of intense activity, he created his own refined cubism (figs. 37–47). In June 1914, he returned to Holland for his first one-man show, and was trapped there by the outbreak of war. Still living a life that was ascetic in both artistic and philosophical terms, he came into contact with a new generation of Dutch artists who appreciated the completely abstract works he was now painting. They included Bart van der Leck and Theo van Doesburg (pp. 23, 24). In 1917, Von Doesburg launched the review *De Stijl* in order to promote the new art Mondrian was, until 1924, its main contributor.

When peace was restored, Mondrian was able to go back to his Paris studio at 26 rue du Départ. It was a small and meticulously arranged space which, throughout the inter-war period, was famous amongst artists (pp. 10, 28, 29). Mondrian had now perfected both the theory and the practice of the art he wanted to promote. Léonce Rosenberg's gallery published his pamphlet *Le Néo-plasticisme* in 1920. In parallel with his plastic work, Mondrian was to write a great deal throughout his life. His collected writings eventually took the form of a very large volume to which we have to make constant reference if we wish to reach a true understanding of his thought processes. Even when the Stedelijk Museum in Amsterdam organized an exhibition of his work to mark his fiftieth birthday, Mondrian was still an artist's artist. He was unknown to the general public and his fame was very slow to spread to other coun-

Portrait of Mondrian, 1907

tries. A monograph on Schelfhout, who was Mondrian's junior, appeared in Germany as early as 1921, but no monographs were published on Mondrian during his own lifetime. In the spring of 1926, the Musée du Jeu de Paume held a major exhibition of more than fifty contemporary Dutch painters. His friends Schelfout, Jan Sluyters, Leo Gestel, and Otto van Rees, who were all younger than Mondrian, were all represented, but not a single work by Mondrian himself was shown, even though he was then living in Paris.

Mondrian lived very modestly by painting commercial subjects (he painted flowers until the mid-1920s) and accepting allowances from a few patrons. He was undemonstrative but, as many people — Léger, Seuphor (p. 43), Arp, Ben Nicholson — can testify, friendship was very important to him. Far from leading a solitary life, Mondrian belonged to many artistic groups; although De Stijl is the best known of these, it should be recalled that he was also a member of Cercle et Carré, Abstraction-Création, and Circle. Being surrounded by friends obviously counted for a great deal during this period of adversity when he had to face the hostility of the general public. Even so, the Nazi threat forced him to leave Paris for London in October 1938. Two years later, the Blitz forced him to flee to New York. On both occasions he took up his work where he had left it off, prepared new publications to explain his painting and his vision of the future, and made new friends. He was still very active before he died early in 1944.

Mondrian in his studio in
Paris, 1933
(Photo: Gemeentemuseum,
The Hague)

Mondrian in his studio in
New York, c. 1942
(Photo: Fritz Glarner,
Collection of Harry
Holtzman)

The need to find some correspondence between the man and his art is such that every possible link has already been established. Mondrian's simple tastes and the sobriety of his studio have been seen as an expression of his Calvinism, whilst his supposedly austere character has been said to be quite in keeping with the sharp-angled chairs that prevented visitors from staying too long (*dixit* Mondrian, who was probably referring to bores), but the joke is at odds with the sociability described by others. A great deal has been made of the taste he always showed for jazz and modern dances, as though it were an inexplicable eccentricity. "In modern dancing (steps, boston, tango, etc.)," he writes, "the curved line of the old dances (waltz, etc.) has yielded to the straight line, and each movement is immediately neutralized by a countermovement — which signifies the search for equilibrium" (*The New Art — The New Life. The Collected Writings of Piet Mondrian*, edited and translated by Harry Holtzman and Martin S. James, London: Thames and Hudson, 1987, p. 43). He told a newspaper that he would never again return to Holland if the Dutch banned the Charleston, as was suggested in 1926. Yet his comment was not so much a defense of a dance as a condemnation of inquisitorial puritanism. And what of it? T. S. Eliot did the fox-trot and sang "Under the Bamboo Tree." Those who knew Edmond Jabès also knew a man with a great fondness for the tango. It is very difficult to draw any conclusion from recreational activities. Mondrian's personality is present in his art, but not in any anecdotal sense (and it should be recalled that Mondrian threw out a journalist who dared to ask him about his private life). The fleeting and charming image of a man dancing the charleston and enjoying his boogie-woogie records tells us all we need to know about the private life of the creator of neo-plasticism.

THE HAGUE SCHOOL

The very mention of Dutch painting brings a number of names to mind: Rembrandt, Vermeer, Pieter de Hooch, Franz Hals, Ruysdael, van Goyen . . . but these are all seventeenth century artists. When one thinks of modern painting, two names immediately spring to mind: Van Gogh and his tormented colour, and then Mondrian with his sober squares. What happened in the intervening two hundred years? Were the two modern painters born in an artistic desert, or was their art nourished solely by influences from outside the Netherlands? The lack of information about the genesis of Mondrian's work may be a source of some disquiet, in that we are talking about a radicalization that has few parallels in the history of painting.

It was only in the 1960s that the Hague school began to be talked about once more, even though it was famous in its own day. Exhibitions were held and studies were published (notably by Jos de Gruyter). Links began to be established between nineteenth-century painters who were almost unknown outside their own country, and the internationally famous Van

Gogh and Mondrian. An exhibition held in Amsterdam in 1980 shed light on Van Gogh's relationship with his elders. Is it a coincidence that since then the Louvre has rehung this painter who was once seen as belonging to the French school alongside the other painters of the Dutch school? At almost the same time, exhibitions which compared the early Mondrian with the Hague school were held in the Netherlands, and then in England, France, Italy, and many other countries.

Shortly after 1870, a group of painters living in The Hague and painting in the same style began to be referred to as the Hague school. The movement had in fact come into being in mid-century when painters like Johannes Bosboom, Willem Roelofs, Paul Gabriel, Jozef Israels, and J. H. Weissenbruch (all of whom were born between 1817 and 1824) began to distance themselves from romanticism; rather than painting vaguely dramatic historical or mythological scenes and characters, they turned to landscapes and rural interiors. A similar but earlier movement influenced by Courbet and the Barbizon school had already led to a reaction against the previous generation's endless versions of *Liberty Guiding the People, Oedipus and the Sphynx* and *Raft of the Medusa*. The painters of the Hague school knew the Barbizon painters; Roelofs had stayed with them on several occasions, and his landscapes are reminiscent of the work of Théodore Rousseau, whilst Israel's landscapes remind one of those of François Millet. The Hague school's impact on Dutch painting was all the stronger and more lasting in that a second generation was able to adopt its aesthetic twenty years later, given that the Dutch had no taste for impressionism. We find the same bucolic inspiration in gifted painters like Anton Mauve (who gave Van Gogh advice) and the Maris brothers (whom Mondrian knew): clusters of trees, cattle in the fields, work on the farm, windmills, rivers, beaches, and boats . . . it was only when he reached the age of forty that Mondrian abandoned these themes (figs. 5–31). His early paintings are even marked by the same fondness for watercolour and black chalk.

Mondrian learned the rudiments of drawing from his father, an amateur painter who made edifying prints with ideological and propagandistic themes, but it was his uncle Frits Mondriaan (1853–1932) who gave him the best

advice on how to become a painter. And his uncle, who was to devote himself exclusively to painting, was a follower of the Hague school. He encouraged his nephew's vocation and took him with him to paint from life, just as his own masters had done. For years, and despite the need to work on nudes and still lifes for the Prix de Rome competition, most of Mondrian's painting were of landscapes and scenes from everyday life. One of the earliest to have been preserved is *Forest and Stream* (fig. 1). Dated 1888, it is executed in charcoal and black chalk, and was probably copied from a print. The slightly later *Young Girl Writing* (c. 1890, fig. 2) is also in black chalk and reveals the same skill. These are, however, no more than academic studies, as are the copies of paintings he made as part of his apprenticeship; in 1895, he copied paintings of the Hague school in the Rijksmuseum, beginning with Gabriël's *In the Month of July*. As for the dozens of sketches, watercolours, and oils Mondrian executed *en plein air* in accordance with the injunctions of the Hague masters, it is often very difficult to situate them accurately within the painter's evolution, as they are not dated. It is not unusual for curators and specialists to attribute widely divergent dates to the works Mondrian painted before 1905. It is true that until this date the painter's development had been very slow and that, at best, he succeeded in equalling the achievements of his uncle, Frits Mondriaan. Although commendable, works like *Evening: Boat on the Amstel* (1900–1902) or *Farm*

Pasture and Willows, 1904
Chalk, charcoal, and stump on paper, 18 1/4 × 22 7/8 in. (46.5 × 58 cm)
Gemeentemuseum, The Hague

(1902–1904) (figs. 5, 7) would not have ensured Mondrian a place in the history of art.

Whether the portrait of the *Young Girl* (fig. 6) dates from 1900–1901 (as H. Holtzman and M. S. James, and R. Welsh suggest) or from 1908 (as M. Seuphor and C. L. Ragghianti argue) does not raise any real problems in that Mondrian rarely executed portraits, and it therefore does not represent a major stage in his evolution. It would, on the other hand, be of great interest if it could be proved that *Woods* (fig. 4) dates from 1898–1900 and not 1906–1907, as that would demonstrate an early desire to escape the Hague school by using unusual colours and framing his subject in a way that recalls the Nabis: the trees are cropped halfway up the trunk and the absence of foliage means that the work is structured by imperious verticals. Given the innovative chromatics and composition, the second date seems more likely, unless, like Michel Seuphor, we adopt the median solution and date it to 1903–1905. The very beautiful *Isolated House* (fig. 3) poses the same problem: curators date it to 1898–1900, whilst Seuphor dates it to 1906–1908. Once again, the care taken over the building's geometry and the absence of any naturalism in the use of the colours, which are drowned by the dominant

blue-green, suggest the later date. This work might be contrasted with *Wood near Oele* (p. 12), while it is comparable with *Farm at Nistelrode* (fig. 10) and *Evening: Sheepfold* (fig. 9), both of which do seem to date from 1904–1906. Writing in *De Stijl* many years later, Mondrian recalled with pleasure the attraction that the architecture of Brabant farmhouses had for him. Recalling the years of his apprenticeship at this late stage in his life, he wrote: "I preferred to paint landscape and houses seen in grey, dark weather or in very strong sunlight, when the density of the atmosphere obscures the details and accentuates the large outlines of objects. I often sketched by moonlight — cows resting or standing immovable on flat Dutch meadows, or houses with dead, blank windows. I never painted these things romantically; but from the very beginning, I was always a realist. Even at this time, I disliked particular movement, such as people in action. I enjoyed painting flowers, not bouquets, but a single flower at a time in order that I might better express its plastic structure. My environment conditioned me to paint the objects of ordinary vision; even at times to make portraits with likeness. For this reason, much of this early work has no permanent value" (*The New Art — The New Life*, p. 338).

Until now, the career of Piet Mondrian — or Mondriaan, as he wrote his name at this time — had been conventional. In accordance with the taste of the day, he painted landscapes with meadows, rivers, windmills, trees, and flowers, or in other words the full repertoire that was expected of Dutch painters. These works were well received, and even found buyers. Mondrian, however, was not satisfied and in about 1907 he began to change. His visit to the Van Gogh retrospective in Amsterdam in 1905 must already have had a considerable intellectual impact: his predecessor's pure colours and very gestural brushwork went against all the principles he had respected to date. Then there were the fauves, who were widely discussed after the sudden revelation of the 1905 Salon d'Automne in Paris. A few canvases by Kees Van Dongen were even shown in Amsterdam. Mondrian would always respect him, despite the aesthetic differences that finally drove them apart. "The first thing to change in my painting was colour. I foresook natural colour for pure colour. I had come to feel that the colours of nature cannot be reproduced on canvas. Instinctively, I felt that painting had to find a new way to express the beauty of nature" (*The New Art — The New Life*, p. 338). The change is obvious in *Evening over the Gein* (1906–1907, fig. 12). The painting depicts a single mass of very dark green: the tree and the reflections in the water stand out against the earth and against the mauvish beige-grey of the sky and its reflection. The painter is no longer concerned with modelling and depth, but with mass effects and simple colour contrasts.

In *Landscape* and *Landscape with Red Cloud* (1907, figs. 15, 16), Mondrian's work bcomes abstract. In one, great streaks of colour sweep across the canvas. In the other, the canvas, divided into two horizontal sectors, is obviously brushed in rapidly to highlight the red area, which, according to the title, is a cloud. From now on, colour is free. This does not mean that the paintings were conceived rapidly. On the contrary, they were the result of long periods of reflection and preparation. *Moonrise on the Banks of the Gein* (1907–1908, fig. 11) marks a return to a place which Mondrian had known for a long time and where he had often set up his easel. The painting derives directly from a large preparatory drawing in charcoal, *Banks of the Gein: Trees by Moonlight* (p. 13). The trees and the details of their branches are carefully picked out in charcoal, as are their reflections in the water. A small figure, painted half-length, can also be seen turning hay in the field. When he turns the drawing into a painting, Mondrian retains the direction of the trunks and the main branches, but eliminates all the other details. Only the five trees remain. They are perpendicularly separated from their reflections by the rectilinear river bank. Yet it is the almost monochrome colour that strikes the viewer rather than the rigourously frontal structure: the sky, the earth, and the river are all red, and even the dark and vigourously painted mass of the trees and the discret moon do not completely escape this invasive redness. In contrast, *Wood near Oele* (1908, fig. 21) is predominantly blue and streaked with fine lines of colour — it might almost be mistaken for a painting by Edvard Munch, who was then at the height of his fame. In order to measure the distance Mondrian has travelled, we have only to compare this painting with the drawing *Wood near Oele* (p. 12) and with the watercolour *Woods*, which were executed a few years earlier. With *Wood near*

On the Banks of the Gein (Trees by Moonlight), 1907–1908
Charcoal,
24³/4 × 29¹/2 in. (63 × 75 cm)
Gemeentemuseum, The Hague

Oele, Landscape with Red Cloud and *Banks of the Gein by Moonlight*, Mondrian reaches a point simultaneously with Munch and the German expressionists of Die Brucke. Yet the spirited brushwork of these works was perhaps too freely lyrical for someone with a temperamental need to work in accordance with rules.

In 1907, Mondrian made the acquaintance of a number of fellow countrymen with a passion for colour: the painters Jan Sluyters, Otto van Rees, and more importantly, the older Jan Toorop (1858–1928), who was working in Domburg in Zeeland where he had gathered a group of young artists around him. Once the leading exponent of a fantastical symbolism influenced by Jugendstil, Toorop finally adopted a pointillist style shortly before the turn of the century. By the time he met Mondrian, his brushwork had become broader, he was no longer using points of colour, and he had adopted the so-called divisionist technique of using small areas of pure colour. In Belgium and Holland this tendency was known as luminism, and was popularized by Theo van Rysselberghe and Toorop respectively. Mondrian was drawn to the scientific aspect of their work and went through a luminist phase between 1908 and 1910, when he was regarded as one of the major representatives of this new aesthetic.

Mondrian was still concentrating on subjects he had been painting for a long time, executing series of trees, windmills, and towers. *The Tree* of 1908 (fig. 25), which in fact looks more like

a cluster of trees, can be regarded as marking a transition towards divisionism. If, as is possible, the work dates from two or three years later, it can also be seen as marking a transition towards cubism: the colour is distributed along the branches in coloured facets in an almost Cézanne-like style. In terms of the "isolated tree" theme which was to preoccupy Mondrian for some years, it is more tempting to linger over the more highly worked o *The Blue Tree* and *The Red Tree* (figs. 19–20), both of which were painted in 1908. *The Red Tree*, with its dazzling red and blue, is the more finished of the two, but *The Blue Tree* is a better example of how Mondrian uses broad brushstrokes to make the colour radiate around the tree and thus makes its presence more dramatic. Recalling his experiments in 1917 at the time when he founded "the new plastic" in *De Stijl*, he said that he had been "more deeply moved by the leafless tree, with its strong articulation of line or plane, than by trees in leaf, where relationship is blurred" (*The New Art — The New Life*, p. 73). For this whole period, the tree was a symbol of the life force. In 1906, the Belgian poet Emile Verhaeren published *La Multiple Splendeur*, a collection of poems heavily influenced by the ideas of Edouard Schuré. Mondrian was equally enthusiastic about Schuré. The collection centres around the poem "L'Arbre," which immediately became famous. "All by itself," writes Verhaeren, "it imposes its enormous and sovereign life / on the plains." The following lines express an optimism shared by Mondrian: "It gives out a great scream that looks / towards the future." Mondrian too saw the tree as a dynamic source for sky and earth.

Like a tree, a windmill has its roots in earth and water, and feeds on space. No matter whether a windmill grinds corn into flour or drains off surplus water, it is a symbol of life, more so in Holland than anywhere else. *Windmill at Evening* and *Windmill by Sunlight* (1908, figs. 17, 18) are depicted at times when either the darkness or the sun make details disappear, and are very different to the mills Mondrian had painted until then in an attempt to capture the subtle play of the light. There is no shading here, but merely *a few small areas of pure colour*, and the light shines out of them. The neo-plasticist Mondrian was less harsh about this kind of canva due to its deliberate use of color, but considered its emotion insufficiently subordinate to expression: "Where natural emotion dominates plastic expression, a work of art always emphatically expresses the tragic. It expresses the

tragic whenever it expresses sorrow or joy, as in the art of Van Gogh'' (*The New Art — The New Life*, p. 54). The function of anti-realist colour is to free us from the tragic.

Mondrian's colour was a little too loud for the taste of the day. Fortunately, his drawings and watercolours of flowers were more subdued. The public did not turn its back on them, and they even brought him modest sums of money. Most of these works depict chrysanthemums and sunflowers, but there are also rhododendrons, dahlias, marigolds, arums, amaryllis, and lilies, usually painted without any context. As he had been painting and drawing flowers since the turn of the century, we can assume that such works was not primarily a source of money, but a real source of pleasure. That Mondrian later had to paint more flowers than he would have liked is equally obvious. At this point in his evolution, his flowers are beautiful graphic studies (p. 15) and they do not yet clash with the rest of his work.

The works painted in Zeeland between 1908 and 1910 (when Toorop was working with a group of young artists) were executed under the sign of luminism. *Zeeland Farmer* (1909–1910, fig. 28) and *Dune II* (1909, fig. 26) are reminiscent of the divisionist techniques Matisse, Derain, and a number of the fauves, including Braque, had been using a few years earlier. The same simple outlines disappear into touches of colour, and they display the same taste for views painted in full sunlight. Yet this dissolution of form into a profusion of colours probably became too excessive for Mondrian's liking. In the views of dunes that he executed later, he abandons luminist brushwork and rediscovers flatness, and also the importance of line, as in *Dune V* (fig. 27), which is contemporary with *Lighthouse at Westkapelle* (1909–1910, figs. 29, 30). In the latter, the great phallic structure soars into the space of the canvas, consuming it. The lines are very clean, but they were as hastily ap-

Chrysanthemum, 1908
Charcoal,
30⁷/₈ × 18¹/₈ in. (78.5 × 46 cm)
Gemeentemuseum,
The Hague

plied as the colour. This produces a total effect, and details disappear, the rapid brushwork concealing the careful preparatory work. Mondrian had been studying the tower for several years. He had painted it a number of times and had made a careful drawing reproducing all the buttresses and ogival windows, which are almost invisible in the painting. Mondrian was gradually rediscovering essential forms. If we look at the cleanly drawn lines of *Landscape with Dunes* (1911, fig. 35) we can see how far Mondrian had come since the early dune paintings of 1909. Having freed colour from all realist constraints, and having mastered it by using it in different ways, Mondrian was now coming to terms with the problem of form.

A SYMBOLIST INTERLUDE

The aesthetic questions Mondrian was asking during this period went hand in hand with a metaphysical quest. Whilst he had renounced the religion of his youth, he had not lost his faith in the spiritual. The second half of the nineteenth century had seen the rise of a fashion for occultism that peaked in the 1880s and 1890s and survived into the present century in a variety of esoteric forms ranging from spiritualism to theosophy. The picturesque wooliness of the most popular manifestations of this occultism must not make us forget that a number of noted intellectuals were able to use it as a springboard for the imagination, including writers such as Victor Hugo with his seance tables, W. B. Yeats, Andrei Biely, and Fernando Pessoa, and musicians like Alexandre Scriabin and Erik Satie — even famous scientists like William Crookes and Camille Flammarion. In terms of our present concerns, it should be noted that several of the great founding fathers of abstract art turned to theosophy or anthroposophy. Vasily Kandinsky refers to Madame Blavatsky in his *Concerning the Spiritual in Art*, whilst Auguste Herbin refers to Rudolf Steiner in his *L'Art non-figuratif non-objectif*.

This interest in every aspect of the occult or the esoteric was a reaction against positivist materialism at a time when it had become impossible to reconcile science and religion; hence the international success of works which attempted to synthesize the two. Madame H. P. Blavatsky was the founder of the Theosophical Society and her *The Secret Doctrine* (1888–1897) is subtitled "A Synthesis of Science, Religion and Philosophy." Schuré's *The Great Initiates*, one of the few books Mondrian kept all his life and throughout all his wanderings, is an attempt to prove that all religions and all beliefs are the expression of a single mystery that was revealed to great initiates like Orpheus, Buddha, and Christ. In similar fashion, Schuré likens science to a new religion and ends the preface thus: "The art of life and all the arts cannot be reborn unless they are in harmony." The artist has a duty to become an initiate (Mondrian was to remember this expression). He must be initiated into the "higher realities of the spirit," into "knowledge of higher worlds" and "the invisible beyond.". Whatever this actually means, it seemed to satisfy a *fin de siècle* that was very partial to sphynxes, chimeras, fairies, and the other evanescent entities depicted by symbolist painters. The Netherlands obviously did not escape this infatuation, and the Theosophical Society had a branch there. What is more, Mondrian could not have failed to hear of Frederick van Eeden, a socialist doctor who was as keen on poetry as he was on esotericism. Be that as it may, Mondrian began to take an interest in these questions at the turn of the century. It was, however, only when his painting entered its modernist phase that his interest in theosophy began to crystalize. We know that he joined the Theosophical Society in 1909. He probably did not remain an orthodox member for many years, but he belonged long enough for it to leave its mark on his painting, and then his writings. His exposition of the principles of neo-plasticism in *De Stijl* in 1917 contains passages like this: "Until now periods of culture arose when a particular individual (above and beyond the people) awakened the universal in the masses. Initiates, saints, deities brought the people, as if from without, to recognize and to feel the universal; and thus to the concept of a pure style," and "The new spirit comes strongly to the fore in *logic, just as in science and religion*. The imparting of veiled wisdom has long yielded to the wisdom of pure reason, and knowledge shows increasing exactness. The old religion with its mysteries and dogmas is increasingly thrust aside by a clear relationship to the universal. That is made possible through purer knowledge of the universal — insofar as it can be known" (*The New Art — The New Life*, pp. 35, 43–44, Mondrian's emphasis). Mondrian was clearly moving beyond Madame Blavatsky's *Isis Unveiled* in the direction of something new, to which he would now devote himself: a new art which must change life. Michel Seuphor sums up his friend's evolution in one sentence: "His Calvinism was replaced by theosophy, then theosophy itself was absorbed (after 1916) by Neo-Plasticism, which for him was to be capable of expressing *everything* without words" (*Piet Mondrian: Life and Work*, London: Thames and Hudson, 1957, p. 58). Such, in a nutshell, were the three stages in Mondrian's spiritual evolution.

The large watercolour entitled *Passion Flower* (fig. 31) dates from 1908–1909. It is probably a visual pun on the similarity between the woman with her eyes closed in ecstasy and the two passion flowers (the stamens and petals are said to represent the instruments of Christ's passion). The perfect symmetry of the figure, which is closely framed by the two flowers, is not very satisfying. Like the large *Nude* study (1908–1911, fig. 32), this may have been a preparatory study for the *Evolution* triptych (fig. 33), but the rounded curves of *Nude* still have a certain sensuality which vanishes completely in the other two works. The whole of the large triptych is based on an imperious symmetry. To the left, there is an almost androgynous woman who is either asleep or absorbed in mystical meditation. She is framed by two symbols which can be read as red arums (not passion flowers) with irregular black triangles in the centre; to the right, there is an identical woman, but she is flanked by stars of David with mystical triangles at their centre. The two women support the central panel, where the same woman serenely stares straight ahead with huge blue eyes. We are supposed to be impressed by this figure who, like some priestess or initiate, is wearing either an Egyptian pschent or an Assyrian headdress. Spheres, triangles, and other all-purpose symbolic figures surround her as she emerges from the intense light of revelation. Its large format and its simplistic "mystery" mean that *Evolution* is visually unsatisfactory. Yves-Alain Bois unkindly refers to it as "that gigantic and mediocre contraption" (*L'Atelier de Mondrian*, Paris: Macula, 1982, p. 29). It is true that, in aesthetic terms, it belongs to a different age: that of the Rose + Croix salons (1892–1897) where distinguished artists and poets mixed with more or less bogus magi. It was, however painted in 1911, and whilst Kandinsky's theosophical speculations may have helped him to free himself from figuration and to found a truly abstract act, Mondrian does not appear to have been ready to do the same. Unlike Kandinsky, Mondrian is in search of the *universal*, not the *spiritual*. He makes the difference quite clear in the "Dialogue on the New Plastic" of 1919: "The *soul*? The sages also speak of the soul of *animals*. It is *spirit* that makes man *man*. But the task of art is to express the *super*human. It is pure expression of the incomprehensible force that is universally active and that we can therefore call *the universal*" (*The New Art — The New Life*, p. 80).

The themes that inspired *Evolution* also inspired several self-portraits in which Mondrian delights in making himself look like an initiate. In the self-portrait of 1908–1909 (p. 17), Mondrian, who may have been thinking of the self-portrait in which Durer depicts himself as Christ, stares at the viewer with huge eyes, as though in an attempt to hypnotise him (hypnotism was very fashionable at this time). The same desire to impress is apparent in *Church in Domburg* (1910–1911, fig. 34). The building is seen in close-up, but no details are visible and the colours are unusual. The red church seems to leap up between the blue foliage and the ground. The red and blue effects and the foreshortened perspective are even more strongly em-

Self-Portrait, 1908–1909
Charcoal and black chalk on brown card,
31 1/8×20 7/8 in. (79×53 cm)
Gemeentemuseum,
The Hague

Church in Domburg,
1908–1909
Ink,
16 3/8×11 in. (41.5×28 cm)
Gemeentemuseum,
The Hague

phasized in *The Red Mill* (fig. 36) of 1911. This is probably the last example of this subject which was dear to Mondrian. In his 1919 "trialogue," he writes: "Indeed, I find this windmill very beautiful. Particularly now that we are too close to it to view it in *normal perspective* and therefore cannot see or draw it *normally*. From here it is very difficult merely to reproduce what one sees: one must dare to try a *freer mode of representation*. In my early work, I tried repeatedly to represent things seen from close by, precisely because of the grandeur they then assume" (*The New Art — The New Life*, p. 99). Here, the monumentality becomes almost ghostly: the body of the mill emerges from the geometrical tracery of the ground and stands out with a visionary clarity. Like the figures in the earlier *Evolution*, it stands in a blue immensity. It is anthropomorphic. In this context, the sails form a huge X in a blue infinity, rather than a cross. Mondrian soon became dissatisfied with these very literary symbols. He saw them as a blind alley or, as he puts it more accurately in "The New Plastic in Painting," "a new limitation" that was just as restrictive as realist painting.

It was probably the discovery of the cubist paintings of Picasso and Braque that put an end to this symbolist interlude. They were shown in the autumn of 1911 at the first exhibition organized by the Cercle d'Art Moderne, which had been founded by Mondrian and some friends to show the most recent tendencies in painting. The surprise they occasioned must have greatly influenced his decision to leave for Paris, where, it seemed, the fate of the art of the future was being decided.

AN UNUSUAL CUBISM

Still Life with Ginger Pot I (1911–1912, fig. 37) seems to have been painted just before Mondrian left for Paris. Prior to this date, it was very unusual for him to paint still lifes (with the exception of the flower paintings). It was probably the example set by Picasso and Braque, who painted many still lifes, that led him to a theme which he could adapt to his own taste. This is the classic reflective theme, and it allowed him to spend as much time as he liked on painting and modelling it. The painting follows the example set by Cézanne in that depth divides the space into planes and flat areas of colour, but it is not radically different from Mondrian's previous work: the objects (a pot, glasses, and a bottle) are drawn clearly and are quite brightly coloured, whereas Picasso and Braque tended at this stage to work in monochromatic ochres or greys. It is, however, the perfectly centred position of the large turquoise pot that reminds one of Mondrian's earlier techniques and paintings. *Still Life with Ginger Pot II* (fig. 39), on the other hand, was executed in Paris and is unambiguously cubist in inspiration. Although the objects are distributed in similar fashion, Mondrian has slightly decentred the pot of ginger, and its round form and the turquoise now help to emphasize both the play of the cleanly drawn lines, most of them horizontal and vertical, and the very muted colours of the work as a whole. A real process of abstraction has taken place: the objects are reduced to contours and we can recognize only the pot, two stewpots, and perhaps a coffee pot.

Mondrian — who now wrote his name with only one "a" — had, then, been converted to cubism with an enthusiasm that he never attempted to minimize. In his view, cubism had taken "the great step toward abstraction." As he put it in a letter written to the critic H. P. Brenner in 1914: "I was influenced by seeing Picasso's work, which I very much admire. I am not ashamed to mention this influence for I think that it is better to hold oneself open to improvements than to remain satisfied with one's imperfection" (*The New Art — The New Life*, p. 15).

Although cubism led Mondrian to simplify his drawing more radically than ever before, it did not change his themes. *Nude* (1911–1912, fig. 38) seems to depict the same figure as *Evolution* but it does so in a very different spirit: a play of planes with almost no depth depicts a very simple geometrical female silhouette which is not so far removed from some cubist paintings, such as Picasso's *The Guitarist* of 1910 (Musée National d'Art Moderne, Paris). As always, Mondrian is more interested in trees and clusters of trees than in the human figure and portraits. *Landscape with Trees* (fig. 40), which is contemporary with *Nude* and the second *Still Life*, is a typical cubist painting based upon the contrast between the angular and rectilinear shapes of the houses, and the ogives formed by the crowns of the trees. This particular form of foliage seems to be the distinguishing sign of the three artists who lived at 26 rue du Départ, as it also appears in the Provençal landscapes painted by Lodewijk Shelfhout in 1912, and in the landscapes Diego Rivera painted in Toledo in 1913. *The Tree* and *Apple-Tree in Blossom* (1912, figs. 41, 42) are much more individual. They are the direct descendents of *The Red Tree* and *The Blue Tree* but they are painted in a very different spirit. The greens, whites, and greys tend to merge into one another, just as they do in the almost monochrome paintings Picasso and Braque executed in 1909–1912. Whereas the tree's foliage once formed an ogive, it is now more diffuse and lends an upward movement (*The Tree*) or a greater spatial expansion (*Apple Tree in Blossom*) to the painting. The lines that extend beyond the painting recall the lines of force the futurists used to dynamize their paintings. The tree eventually disappears almost completely, and becomes no more than a pretext for an abstract composition, as in *Composition: Trees II* (1912–1913, fig. 43) and *Oval Composition (Trees)* (1913, fig. 48). The latter, which marks the final dislocation of analytic cubism, is a magnificent assemblage of black lines on grey and yellow ochre, and adopts the oval format reintroduced by Braque and Picasso from 1910 onwards. This time, Mondrian is as abstract as they are — one thinks, for example, of Braque's very similar *Violonist* (1911: Fondation Buhrle, Zurich). Mondrian presumably reworked the sketches and watercolours executed in Domburg to produce these new compositions. They include the astonishing *Composition of Lines and Colours (Windmill)* (1913, fig. 46), which is Mondrian's final windmill. This time, the greater density of small rectangles is enough to suggest the presence of the cross made by the sails in a space that has almost no depth.

Guillaume Apollinaire, who saw this analytic cubism at the 1913 Salon des Indépendants, clearly grasped its originality and even guessed that Mondrian would take a very different path to that followed by his main sources of inspiration (we know that Braque's first *papiers collés* and Picasso's first collages, which the poet described as "research into matter," date from 1912). "Although his work derives from that of the cubists, Mondrian does not imitate them. He seems to have been influenced primarily by Picasso, but his personality remains his own. His trees and his portrait of a woman reveal a sensible cerebralism. This cubism is following a different path to the one being taken by Braque

Untitled (Oval Composition), 1914
Charcoal on paper, 60×39 3/8 in. (152.5×100 cm)
Peggy Guggenheim Collection, Venice
Photograph © The Solomon R. Guggenheim Foundation

and Picasso, whose research into matter is of such interest at the moment" (*Œuvres en prose complètes*, Paris: Gallimard, 1991, p. 535). And it is quite true that Mondrian's work would not lead to an interest in texture or *papiers collés*. He was to confine himself strictly to the painted canvas.

Dutch towns, with their gabled houses with mullioned windows, belonged to another age. Mondrian was astonished by the brutal geometry of the streets of Paris, the shameless display of advertising on the walls, and the anarchy of the roofs and chimneys he could see from his studio window. All this was perfectly in keeping with the way he had been making his subjects more geometrical ever since he had moved to Paris. In 1913, apartment buildings and scaffolding begin to appear in his work, and at the same time colour, which he had used sparingly when he was still under the influence of Braque and Picasso, gradually begins to return. The change begins with *Composition VII* (1913, fig. 45) and then continues in a series of deliberately oval paintings which emphasize the straight lines and angles of the composition. At the same time, the curves and oblique lines tend to disappear, as in *Oval Colour Planes* (1913–1914; fig. 49), *Oval Composition III* (1914, fig. 47) and *Oval Composition in an Oval: KUB* (1914, fig. 50). Whilst

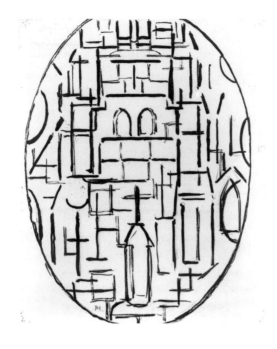

colour — usually blues, pinks and ochres — tends to be solid and contained within the geometrical graphic figures, the paintings make no attempt to produce the illusion of depth. Mondrian is, however, still abstracting from real objects, a few traces of which suggest the arches of lintels or an advertisement for Kub stock cubes — the cubists found this slogan very amusing, and Picasso in particular used it on several occasions in 1912. Mondrian has gone beyond analytic cubism to the extent that he is now freely redistributing residual elements of the real model he is using as a pretext, and turning them into a visual composition which makes no reference to the everyday world. Mondrian had reached this point by the beginning of 1914, when he explained to H. P. Brenner: "I construct complexes of lines and colours on a flat plane so as to plastically express *universal beauty* — as consciously as possible. Nature (or the visible) inspires me, arousing in me the emotion that stimulates creation, no less than with any other painter, but I want to approach truth as closely as possible; I therefore abstract everything until I attain the essential of things . . . With the use of horizontal and vertical lines constructed *consciously* but without calculation, under the guidance of higher intuition, and brought to harmony and rhythm with these elements of beauty — supplemented where necessary by lines in other directions or by curved lines — I think that one can create a work of art as strong as it is true" (*The New Art — The New Life*, p. 14). The

new emphasis Mondrian places on the conscious and deliberate process of creation dates from this period. Writing in *De Stijl* in 1919, he made his intentions quite clear: "I said '*art* is intuition'; the expression of art must be conscious. Only when the mind consciously discerns the true nature of intuition can intuition act purely. . . Only *conscious* man can purely mirror the universal: he can *consciously* become one with the universal and so can *consciously* transcend the individual" (ibid., p. 80).

Mondrian was visiting Holland when the Great War broke out. Cut off from his Paris studio and his work in progress, he tried to go on with his research. *The Sea* (1914, p. 21) is a direct continuation of the last works he executed in Paris. Mondrian was probably not satisfied with it; it seemed to him that he had to go still further. In an autobiographical text written in 1941, he was to recall: "Gradually, I became aware that Cubism did not accept the logical implications of its own discoveries; it was not developing abstraction towards its ultimate goal, the expression of pure reality" (*The New Art — The New Life*, p. 338). The cubists had now abandoned the multiple perspectives of analytic cubism, and were confining their paintings to the two dimensions of the object-plane, but neither Picasso nor Braque took the further step of abandoning all reference to objects and expressing only a purely abstract reality. Mondrian worked through the entire spectrum of the formal expressions of the day, from the Barbizon-style realism of the Hague school to impressionism and symbolism and then to cubism; like his contemporary Malevich, he would always stress that experimentation played an important part in his evolution. For the moment, he was reflecting as he stared at the sea, a subject which, it seemed to him, held the solution to his aesthetic problems. He hesitated for months and some commentators like L. J. F. Wijsenbeek even think that he reverted to figuration for some commissions *Farm at Duivendrecht* (fig. 51) or even *Windmill by Moonlight*, both of which can be dated to 1915–1916, may be cases in point. Assuming these commentators to be correct, Mondrian was not the only one to do so at this time: Picasso drew some very "lifelike" portraits from 1915 onwards and Severini painted a realist *Mother and Child* in 1916. The supposed interlude did not, however, prevent him from thinking.

It is possible that Mondrian missed the stimulation provided by Parisian artistic circles, though he was not a great enthusiast for intellectual gatherings. In 1914, he spent some time in Domburg with Toorop's circle of artists, but he now found Toorop very dated. Even Jacoba van Heemskerck, who had a talent for "cubizing" was out of step with his new frame of mind. He therefore moved to Laren, a village some thirty kilometers from Amsterdam, where he found a small but more stimulating intellectual community. Its most important members were the composer Jacob von Domselaer and the mystical philosopher M. H. J. Schoenmaekers. Of the very few works painted in 1915–1916, the most interesting are the sharply contrasting *Composition No. 10* (1915, fig. 52) and *Composition 1916* (fig, 57) (it should be noted in passing that the painter was again writing his name with two "a"s). The former concludes the series of drawings begun with *The Sea* (1914, p. 21) and tranposes the antithetical dynamics of the ocean and a pier that plunges extended verticals. into the horizontal movement of the waves. Both are dissolved into a pattern of orthogonal black signs scattered across a grey ground: there is no more colour, no more oblique lines, and no more curves, with the exception of the oval which all the signs form within the space of the painting. In 1941, Mondrian was to describe his experiments thus: "More and more I excluded from my painting all curved lines, until finally my compositions consisted only of vertical and horizontal lines, which formed crosses, each one separate and detached from the other. Observing sea, sky and stars, I sought to indicate their plastic function through a multiplicity of crossing verticals and horizontals. Impressed by the vastness of nature, I was trying to express its expansion, rest, and unity. At the same time, I was fully aware that the visible expansion of nature is at the same time its limitation; vertical and horizontal lines are the expression of two opposing forces; these exist everywhere and dominate everything; their reciprocal action constitutes 'life'" (*The New Art — The New Life*, p. 339). Mondrian's fascination with the bipolarity of vertical and horizontal, positive and negative, and masculine and feminine, which had now been apparent for some years, was to prove a lasting one. *Composition 1916* (fig. 57) is based on the same system, but is far from being monochrome. The way the very intense colour

slides between the black lines demonstrates that Mondrian had not abandoned chromaticism, though for anyone who is familiar with Mondrian's future evolution towards clearly delineated flat areas of colour, it may seem to make a backward step compared with the *Oval Composition III* of 1914 (fig. 47).

Both these compositions express doubts on Mondrian's part. As at every turning point in his evolution, his mood was one of intense introspection and he was filling whole notebooks with his reflections. Mondrian obviously always enjoyed writing, but he was also driven to write by his desire to clarify the aesthetic he could glimpse in his painting and by the encouragement he received from the new acquaintances he made. The most important was Theo van Doesburg, a young painter and architect Mondrian met in 1915 as a result of the enthusiastic article Van Doesburg had written on his work. Van Doesburg was planning to publish a review and wanted Mondrian to expound his ideas in it. In Laren, Mondrian also had as his neighbour the theosophist Schoenmaekers, who published his *Het nieuwe wereldbeeld* "The New Image of the World" in 1915 and his *Beinselen der Beeldende Wiskunde* "Principles of Plastic Mathematics" in 1916. Both works deal with the secret structure of the universe. Certain commentators have made much of Schoenmaeker's supposedly catalysing role in the formation of *De Stijl*. There may be some truth in this. It should, however, be noted that Mondrian gives him no particular importance in his writings. He cites him once or twice, but no more often than, for example, the Hegelian philosopher G. J. P. J. Bolland. As for the expression neo-plasticism, which Mondrian supposedly borrowed from Schoenmaekers, it is not particularly original, and Mondrian, like any other innovative painter, could have invented it without his help. It should be recalled that Mondrian insisted — as did Kandinsky, Kupka, and Malevitch — that his theories developed out of his practice and that we therefore have to look at his plastic works rather than a forgotten esoteric philosopher. As it happens, Mondrian himself provides a clue to his evolution when he mentions the influence of the painter Bart van der Leck, whom he met in 1916. "Van der Leck — while still working figuratively — painted in unified planes and pure colours. My more or less Cubist, therefore more or less painterly technique, was influenced by his exact technique" (*The New Art — The New Life*, p. 182). When one looks at the paintings Bart van der Leck executed in 1914-1916, it seems surprising that their conspicuously naive stylization should have caught Mondrian's attention, even if it was only the clearly delineated silhouettes and the flat colour that interested him. It is probable that he was much more interested in the *Compositions* (p. 23) in which, from 1916 onwards, van der Leck perfects a system of abstraction by simplifying and stylizing the general lines of his subject and reducing it to a small number of narrow bands of colour that form perfect parallelograms. The bands of colour are distributed across a equally solid ground and the titles are the only reminders of the initial model, as in *Composition 1916 (Mine Triptych)* and *Composition 1917 (Dog Cart)*. Van der Leck's reliance on an initial model was, however, soon to signal a fundamental difference from Mondrian's abstraction, which made no allusion to real objects.

Real objects can still be seen in *Composition in Black and White* (fig. 56), which Mondrian began in late 1916. The painting is the final outcome of the "pier and sea" theme he had been working on since his return to Holland, even though the arrangement of the plus and minus signs now makes it impossible to imagine the presence of a pier. The proliferation of signs produces an impressionist flickering effect which the painter found no more satisfactory than an overly conventional centred focalization. The great difference between this and Mondrian's previous works is the new rigour. The lines are perfectly rectilinear and the geometrical forms they trace are orthogonal. The right angle alone governs the forms and relations between them; the colour is solid and there is no shading.

DE STIJL

A turning point had been reached. Mondrian's work and career were entering a new phase. He was no longer alone: van Doesburg had designated him the leader of a new art, a new style and Mondrian was free to express his ideas in the pages of the art journal he launched in 1917 — *De Stijl* (p. 23).

The presence of the small black lines indicates that *Colour Plane Composition A* (1917) is still derivative of *Composition in Black and White*, and the overlapping of some of the planes even suggests a certain depth. The painting tends, however, to escape from the central composition by sliding upwards towards the point where the two planes are divided into sections. This is more obvious in *Colour-Plane Composition No. 3* (1917, fig. 55). The black lines have disappeared. The colour planes spill out of the sides of the painting at several points, but they never overlap. The painting no longer has anything to do with cubism; it is neither centred nor based on symmetry. Indeed, the peripheral areas are just as busy as the centre. Neo-plasticism is born. As though to signal the fact that he is entering a new period, Mondrian now signs his paintings soberly, using only his initials. He also executed a curious *Self-Portrait* (1918, fig. 53) at this time. It is unusually realistic and is an obvious farewell that draws a line under a whole period in his life and work. The self-portrait itself is indeed realistic, but Mondrian places it in front of one of his most radically abstract paintings of 1917, and they signal the birth of neo-plasticism.

In the course of 1918–1919, Mondrian painted his first diamond-shaped painting. To be more specific, it is a square with the horizontals and verticals placed at a diagonal to the viewer (figs. 58, 59). For the first time, he also began to use the grid system that was to become the distinguishing feature of his paintings. His main concern was now to perfect the grid. For the moment, the question of colour, which is used discreetly here, is secondary. Mondrian is still reluctant to make the grid uniform. In some cases, the colour varies from black to grey; in others, its thickness varies — in *Composition in Black and Grey* the more emphatic line upsets the perfectly geometrical lattice, and one thinks of the works of Victor Vasarely and the kinetic artists of later decades.

In 1919 Mondrian executed two other paintings based upon the same subdivision of the canvas into two equal parts. One of the *Checkerboard Compositions* (fig. 61) uses dark colours, and the other light colours. Both consist of two hundred and fifty-six (16 × 16) rectangles of colour. The second composition uses what were to became the basic colours of neoplasticism — the "noncolours" black and white, and the colours blue, yellow, and red, but it is true that Mondrian is still not using pure colour. The absolutely regular division of the space of the painting destroys any impressionist effect.

Composition: Bright Colours with Grey Lines (fig. 60) also dates from 1919. Mondrian was now back in Paris, and working in his studio in the rue du Départ. He now abandons the regular geometrical division of the surface. The grey grid that isolates the spaces of pale colour — whites, beiges or various shades of grey — is irregular and obviously extends beyond the painting. In *Composition with Red, Blue and Yellow-green* (1920, fig. 62), in contrast, the grid does not quite reach the edge of the canvas. Was Mondrian's ultimate goal a colourist effect rather

than a composition balanced by a solid grid and pure colours? Before long, Mondrian was restricting himself to three primary colours, and eventually left them pure, but the grid was to cause him problems at the beginning of the 1920s. Momentarily tempted by a grid of slender lines, as in *Large Composition A* (1920, fig. 64), he finally adopted highly visible lines, usually in black. Until 1923, however, the lines are not usually extended to infinity, and some stop several centimeters short of the edge of the painting, as in several of the fine *Compositions with Red, Yellow and Blue* executed in 1921 and 1922 (figs. 66, 72).

Mondrian now knew that his plastic system was complete, and confidently entitled a perfect work executed in 1921 *Tableau no. 1* (fig. 67). He was now using colours more sparely, but also with greater authority. He was handling space freely and was not afraid to divide it into only a small number of sectors. A large white square imposes its monumentality on certain of the *Compositions with Red, Yellow and Blue* of 1922 (figs. 70, 72), despite the reduced format. In other paintings, in contrast, a very large colour plane spreads over several sectors of the grid, as in *Composition with Large Blue Plane* (1921, fig. 69).

During the crucial years in which Mondrian was perfecting his "new plastic" (he began to speak of neo-plasticism in 1920) he explained his method and clarified his intentions in several essays written in Dutch for *De Stijl*, and then in essays written in French. The most important are "The New Plastic in Painting," which was published in *De Stijl* in 1917 and 1918, "Natural Reality and Abstract Reality: A Trialogue" (1919) and the pamphlet entitled *Le Néo-Plasticisme*

MAANDBLAD GEWIJD AAN DE MODERNE BEELDENDE VAKKEN EN KULTUUR RED. THEO VAN DOESBURG.

VILMOS HUSZAR
Cover design for *De Stijl*,
1917–1920

BART VAN DER LECK
Geometrical Composition 1,
1917
Oil on canvas,
37 3/8 × 40 1/8 in. (95 × 102 cm)
Rijksmuseum Kröller-Müller,
Otterlo

23

(1920). He also expressed his views in articles and reviews whenever the opportunity arose.

In addition to Mondrian and van Doesburg, the De Stijl group included Bart van der Leck (who would drift away from the others in 1920), Vilmos Huszar (p. 23), the Belgian sculptor Georges Vantongerloo, and the architects Robert van't Hoff, J. J. P. Oud, Jan Wils, and Gerrit Rietveld. The first issue of their journal, published in October 1917, opens with a declaration asserting that: "The truly modern — i.e. conscious — artist has a double vocation; in the first place, to produce the purely plastic work of art, in the second place to prepare the public's mind for this purely plastic art . . . By the mere fact that the modern artist is enabled to write about his own work, the prejudice that the modern artist works according to preconceived theories will disappear. On the contrary, it will appear that the new work of art does not derive from theories accepted *a priori*, but rather the reverse, that the principles arise out of creative activity" (Hans L. C. Jaffé, *De Stijl*, London: Thames and Hudson, 1970, p. 10). We can recognize here a number of ideas that Mondrian held dear, and especially the emphasis on the conscious activity of the artist that led De Stijl to oppose all romantic tendencies, including surrealism.

Responding to the frequent criticism that he was no lover of nature, Mondrian argues in his "trialogue" of 1919 that, given that nature is perfect, there is no need to copy it: "Nature is perfect, but man does not need perfect nature in art, precisely because nature is so perfect.

What he does need is a representation of the more inward" (*The New Art — The New Life*, p. 92). This "inwardness" is not something that is reflected in a copy of a fragment of nature: "In art, the universal is impossible to express determinately within naturalistic form" (ibid., p. 107) Hence the need for a non-figurative and simplified art based upon relations of plastic equivalence. Mondrian defines its goals as follows: "To express plastically colour and line means to establish opposition through colour and line; and this opposition expresses plastic relationship. Relationship is what I have always sought, and that is what all painting seeks to express" (ibid., p. 76).

In his very first essay on "Neo-Plasticism in Painting" (1917) Mondrian defines the perpendicularity of lines and planes as the basic means that will allow the new art to eliminate naturalistic confusion: "The New Plastic manifests this insight through the perpendicular duality of its plastic means (In naturalistic painting, female and male elements are confused — in form.)" (*The New Art — The New Life*, p. 67). Mondrian readily takes up the vertical-male / horizontal-female analogy and refuses to tolerate obliques, not to mention curves. "The search for the expression of vastness led to the search for the greatest tension: the straight line; because all curvature resolves into the straight, no place remains for the curved" (ibid., p. 77). On the other hand, no element of mathematical calculation ever enters into any of Mondrian's paintings, and he had disagreements over this point with his friend Vantongerloo. For Mondrian, the positioning of a line, and the dimension of a plane were determined by the eye, intuitively, and mathematics had "nothing to do with the creation of free rhythm in art" (ibid., p. 23).

It is somewhat surprising to find Mondrian asserting in his first text (1917) that painting "must rely upon the three primary colours, supplemented by white, black and grey . . . primary colour only signifies colour appearing in its most basic aspect. Primary colour thus appears very relative — the principal thing is that colour is free of individuality and individual sensations, and that it expresses only the serene emotion of the universal" (*The New Art — The New Life*, p. 36). These words sum up Mondrian's art. And yet we know that when he wrote this he was not yet using only those colours. The paintings of 1917 use muted colours and pastel tones. He explained why this was the case in a letter written to van Doesburg in February 1917: "For the moment, I am using muted colours so as to adapt to the external world; this does not mean that I would not prefer a purer colouration. Otherwise, it might be thought that I was contradicting myself in my work." It was not until 1921 that Mondrian became bold enough to use only primary colours and to apply them unmixed and unemotionally.

Mondrian very quickly realized that all the efforts he was making were an attempt to eliminate his own sensibilities in order to discover universals, and that all the art of the future would have to assert universality, as opposed to individuality. As early as 1915, he wrote in a letter to Augusta de Meester-Obreen: "When we show things in their outwardness (as they *ordinarily* appear), *then* indeed we allow the human, the individual to manifest itself. But when we plastically express the inward (through the abstract form of the outward), then we come closer to manifesting the spiritual, therefore the divine, the universal" (*The New Art — The New Life*, p. 15). Mondrian soon abandoned this residually theosophical language and proclaimed in *De Stijl* in 1917 that: "Only when the individual no longer stands in the way can universality be purely manifested. Only then can universal consciousness (intution) — wellspring of all the arts — express itself directly; and a purer art arises" (ibid., p. 30). And yet I wonder if the old terminology about the male-female dialectic is not somewhat suspect when Mon-

drian writes that the "old plastic" is doomed because it expresses the dominance of the female-external-capricious-mat erialist, whereas neo-plasticism will be based, if not on the predominance of the maculine-inner-straight-spiritual, at least on a balance between the two: "By viewing the expressions of art historically, we see most clearly that the old mentality not only contained impure masculinity, but also that it was dominated by the outward (immature) female. We see this in the plastic expression itself as well as in the *representation* (or *subject matter*). In naturalistic painting, plastic expression was predominantly female outwardness, for natural colour and the capricious undulating line were employed as the expressive means" (ibid., p. 69). There is, according to Mondrian, a direct link between femininity and the expression of the tragic that characterizes all the art of the past and that resists the advent of neo-plasticism: "Art has the *intention* of plastically establishing complete freedom from the tragic, but its *expression*, the *plastic* created by and for man, lags behind art's intention" (ibid., p. 53). In Mondrian's view, anything to do with sentiment, pathos, sensibility and sentimentality is tragic; anything that is opposed to the new art is therefore tragic. His friends on *De Stijl* were in full agreement with him. In the third issue of the journal (January 1918), J. J. P. Oud, for instance, writes: "Paradoxically, it may be said that the struggle of the modern artist is a struggle against feeling. The modern artist strives to attain the universal, while feeling (the subjective) leads to the particular. The subjective is the arbitary, the unconscious, the relatively indeterminate" (Jaffé, *De Stijl*, p. 96). And yet, insists Mondrian, the new mentality must "annihilate the old mentality and domination by the individual, natural (or female) element" (*The New Art — The New Life*, p. 57). He returned to this point in the pamphlet he published in Paris in 1920, and it is not devoid of a embarrassing misogyny: "A Futurist manifesto proclaiming hatred of *woman* (the feminine) is entirely justified. The *woman* in *man* is the direct cause of the domination of the tragic in art" (ibid., p. 137). The abolition of the tragic and the individual therefore involves, according to Mondrian a new balance between the masculine and the feminine in both art and society.

A rejection of all individualist solutions in art and in all social manifestations is characteristic of the *De Stijl* artists. As J. J. P. Oud puts it in the January 1918 issue of the journal: "Great art stands in a causal relationship with the social striving of the age. The longing to make the individual subservient to the social is to be found in everyday life as well as in art, reflected in the need to organize individual elements into groups, associations, confederations, companies, trusts, monopolies, etc. This parallelism of intellectual and social striving which is a necessity for culture forms the basis for style" (Jaffé, *De Stijl*, p. 97). Or as van Doesburg puts it, writing in *De Stijl* in February 1922: "The problem of art occupies a prominent position beside the problem of the economic reconstruction of Europe. I do not propose to go into the question of how far the two problems are interrelated; the only thing that we can be sure of is that the solving of the economic problem, like that of the artistic problem, is beyond the abilities of any one individual, and this fact is an advantage. Because it means that the pre-eminence of the individual, the Renaissance view of life, has come to an end" (ibid., p. 148). Van Doesburg was also the author of the third manifesto "Towards a New World Plasticism" in which artists are described as rising above ideologies, which are all bankrupt, to rebuild the world: "We know only one thing: only the bearers of the (new) spirit are upright . . . We know that those who join us belong from the beginning to the new spirit. With them alone does the spirtual body of the new world permit itself to be formed. Work!" (ibid., p. 147). This hope, which he shared with his friends, allowed Mondrian to dream of a great neo-plasticist utopia. He was already thinking of it in his 1919 "trialogue": "Pure plastic vision must construct a new society, just as it has constructed a new plastic in art — a society where equivalent duality prevails between the material and the spiritual, a society of equilibriated relationship" (*The New Art — The New Life*, p. 99).

THE NEO-PLASTIC ENVIRONMENT

Mondrian always took a particular interest in architecture, hence the many steeples, windmills, towers, and apartment blocks that inspired his early career. He regarded architecture as the most objective of all the arts and was encouraged by modern architecture's tendency towards impersonality: "It is so heartening that the new rational architecture, under the pressure of the practical demands of our time and inspired by new materials, virtually excludes the expression of subjective feeling" (*The New Art — The New Life*, p. 303). That architecture should merge with the absolute painting that Mondrian had perfected was self-evident. In 1917, he deplored the fact that this was not yet possible: "Insofar as the time is not yet ripe for the complete unification of architecture, the new plastic must continue to be manifested as painting" (ibid., p. 37). Three years later, he expressed a more confident view in his pamphlet *Le Néo-plasticisme*: "The future of the New Plastic and its true realization in painting lies in *chromoplastic in architecture*. It governs the interior as well as the exterior of the building and includes everything that plastically expresses relationships through colour. . . . It is *entirely new painting* in which all painting is resolved, pictorial as well as decorative" (ibid., pp. 137–138). Chromo-plasticism abolishes the notion of decorative art, and in fact aspires to encompass every form of art.

Throughout his writings, Mondrian devoted great effort to stressing how important neo-plasticism is to the other arts, and especially drama and music. Like other great founding fathers of abstract art (Kandinsky, Kupka, and Klee), Mondrian often compares painting with music. Without going into the detailed discussion this calls for, we will simply note that his preference is for futurist music (mainly because it rejects melody, which is likened to figuration in art, and results in a certain mechanization of the performance) and jazz (which he liked not for its simple syncopated rhythms and the way it allows musicians to improvise, which was why it appealed to Kupka, but because the charleston, the fox-trot, and the two-step allowed dancers to use perpendicular steps and movements). It was, however, the fusion with architecture that meant most to him. Recapitulating the general principles of neo-plasticism in painting (rectangular planes, primary colours and non-colours), he established an equivalent system for architecture: "In architecture, empty space can be counted as noncolour, denaturalized material as colour" (ibid., p. 214). In his most important essay on chromoplasticism, "The Realization of Neo-Plasticism in the Distant Future and in Architecture Today," which appeared in *De Stijl* in the spring of 1922, Mondrian extends the notion of architecture to the environment: "Architecture, sculpture, painting, and decorative art will . . . merge, that is to say, become *architecture-as-our-environment.*" And when all the other arts (music, dance, drama, literature) merge, there will be no reason for them to have an autonomous existence: "the movement of life itself will become harmonious" and we will dwell in beauty. "But it will be a different beauty from the one we now know, difficult to conceive, impossible to describe . . . *The Neo-Plastic conception will go far beyond art in its future realization*" (ibid., p. 168). The optimism of this vision leaves one quite speechless.

In the early 1920s, a number of artists reached the conclusion that easel painting was making no progress and that the world of galleries and collectors was definitely too restricted and too remote from life. In late 1923, *Le Bulletin de l'Effort moderne*, which was published by Mondrian's dealer Léonce Rosenberg, launched an opinion poll asking the best-known painters of the day "Where is modern painting going?" Most had no idea and gave very evasive answers, with the exception of Gino Severini who predicted that "Visual art will move away from the easel and on to the wall, and will once again become part of the vast environment of architecture" (Severini, *Ecrits sur l'art*, Paris: Cercle d'Art, 1987, p. 22). Severini was thinking of murals, frescoes, and mosaics. Mondrian, however, went so far as to argue that painting as we know it was doomed to vanish: "Neoplasticism is preparing its end. The ultimate consequence of this *pure plastic of relationship* will be painting's transition to plastic realization in our material environment" (*The New Art — The New Life*, p. 193). As he awaited the end of art in a harmonious future for which neither art nor society were ready, Mondrian went on working.

Mondrian worked at his easel, but he also worked on various experiments that took him out of the studio. In 1926, he was commis-

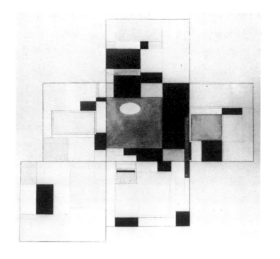

Maquette for *Salon de Mme B à Dresde* (exploded box plan), 1926
Ink and gouache,
29 1/2 × 29 3/4 in.
(74.8 × 75.6 cm)
Staatlichen Kunstsammlung, Kupferstich-Kabinett, Dresden

sioned to make a maquette for *Salon de Mme. B. à Dresde* (figs. 78, 79). The space he was asked to decorate was not ideal because there were openings in the centre of one wall, but Mondrian skillfully positioned his rectangular colour planes in an attempt to displace them optically and to make the viewer forget their central position. One of the commission's other requirements was for an oval table, but in the final version it emphasizes the rectangles painted on the walls, the floor, and the ceiling by introducing a formal contrast. The design, which could have have been impressive, was unfortunately never realized. This was the only occasion on which Mondrian worked for an individual client. It has been assumed that it was because nothing concrete came of the project that Mondrian did not repeat the experiment. I do not take that view: Mondrian was not a man to be discouraged so easily. Although he allowed the designs to be published, he must have been quickly disillusioned with a work that by no means lived up to his hopes. An important text written in 1926 reveals the extent to which a project intended for only one person fell short of his dream: "I have always fought the individualist in man and have tried to show the value of seeing in a universal way; but this does not mean I believe in full collectivism for the present. That is the dream of the future" (*The New Art — The New Life*, p. 207). Until such time as the age was ready for the "collectivist dream," the main task was, according to Mondrian, the elimination of nature. Every part of a building had to be reduced to straight lines and right angles, and all colours had to disappear, with the exception of the three primaries and the three non-colours.

Texture too had to be eradicated. "Surfaces will be smooth and bright, which will also relieve the heaviness of the material. This is one of the many cases where Neo-Plastic art agrees with hygiene, which demands smooth, easily cleaned surfaces" (ibid., p. 211). The white-tiled surfaces designed a few decades later by Jean-Pierre Raynaud had an aesthetic and not a hygenic purpose. The clinical atmosphere is in fact reminiscent of the rational and aseptic socialist paradises typified by Vladimir Mayakovski's *The Bedbug* and *Bathhouse*. But for a systematic dreamer like Mondrian, denaturalising houses alone was not enough. "The truly evolved human will no longer attempt to bring beauty, health or shelter to the city's streets and parks by means of trees and flowers. *He will build healthy and beautiful cities by opposing buildings and empty spaces in an equlibriated way*. Then the outdoors will satisfy him as much as the interior" (ibid., p. 207). We shall discuss later Mondrian's paradoxical treatment of trees and flowers. This stark orthogonal utopia is far too reminiscent of dreary suburbs, of rows of tower blocks like over-perfect parallelepipeds and of empty concrete squares, to inspire any enthusiasm today. Mondrian had no doubt seen too many slums and sordid alleys not to want to make man happy — without consulting him. "And man? Nothing in himself, he will be part of the whole; and losing his petty and pathetic individual pride, he will be happy in the Eden he will have *created!*" (ibid., p. 212). Man will, despite himself, replace the creator. A curious utopia!

The second experiment of 1926 related to a stage set. Michel Seuphor had written *L'Éphémère est éternel* ("The Ephemeral is Eternal"), which is subtitled "Theatrical demonstrations in three actions and two interludes with choruses and ballets," and Mondrian agreed to make a maquette for it, using neo-plastic prin-

ciples (figs. 80, 82). It may seem surprising that Mondrian should have chosen this play for his first and only theatrical venture, as it is much closer to the synthetic futurist drama than to the more contemporary dada or surrealist theatre. Yet, quite apart from his friendship with Seuphor, Mondrian often expressed a certain sympathy for Italian futurism, mainly because he shared its desire to do away with the past. Far from being disconcerted by the futurist aspects of *L'Éphémère est éternel*, Mondrian seems to have liked its impersonality — the absence of any meaning or plot, the onomatopoeia, and the mime. Since his return to Paris, he had also become acquainted with Enrico Prampolini and especially Luigi Russolo, whose *bruitist* music interested him. Even so, there is a discrepancy, which may have appealed to Mondrian, between the play's many, very talkative characters, and the calm set that surrounds them. The set consists of a shallow paralleliped, with the open side facing the audience and set inside a rectangle which also faces the audience. The only element to change from one "action" to the next is the backdrop and another parallelepiped which is inverted and moved. The maquette was never executed during Mondrian's lifetime, but he does seem to have been satisfied with an experiment that gave a concrete expression to some of the suggestions put forward in "Neo-Plasticism: Its Realization in Music and Future Theatre," which appeared in *De Stijl* in 1922. He imagines a hall built and painted in accordance with neo-plasticist principles, in which the audience can come and go at will to hear music or watch spectacles and paintings. "In short, the hall will be neither a theatre nor a church, but a spatial construction satisfying all the demands of beauty and utility, matter and spirit. No ushers or staff: an automatic buffet, or better yet no buffet at all, for one might leave the building without missing anything. Indeed, compositions could be repeated, just as modern cinemas schedule the same film at stated times. There could be long intermissions: for those who stay the interval could be filled by Neo-Plastic paintings. When it becomes technically possible, these could also appear as projected images. Artists and sponsors will no longer have to devise endless variations of programme or to hunt for something 'novel' " (*The New Art — The New Life*, p. 163). This is, in short, the old dream of a total art available to all which achieves such

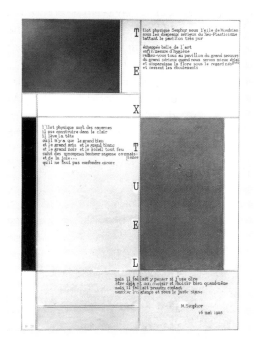

a level of perfection that there is no need to look for anything new. Art thus merges into ritual.

In his 1919 "trialogue," Mondrian argues that it is inconceivable for an artist to work on "a new concept of beauty" (*The New Art — The New Life*, p. 109) in an antiquated environment. It was at this point that he began to make his working environment mirror his plastic research. The furniture created by the artist and the coloured rectangles he painted or suspended from the ceiling could all be moved around, and their form, size and colour, could be changed to suit the mood of the moment and, more importantly, the work in progress on the easel. Everything had to be in harmony with the work in progress, and had to form a visually pleasing whole (pp. 28, 29). Mondrian wanted a precise and intimate relationship between container and content, or in other words, between the room and the furniture that was specially designed for it. He explains his principles at length in the seventh "scene" of his "trialogue" and stresses that "Everything has to be designed in accordance with *the one idea, the New Plastic conception*, if pure equilibriated relationship is to be exactly expressed in the whole" (ibid., p. 111). The results have often been described by those who visited Mondrian's studio. Seuphor, for example, describes it in these terms: "The room was quite large, very bright, with a very high ceiling. Mondrian had divided it irregularly, utilizing for

this purpose a large black-painted cupboard, which was partially hidden by an easel long out of service; the latter was covered with big grey and white paste-boards. Another easel rested against the large rear wall whose appearance changed often, for Mondrian applied to its his Neo-Plastic virtuosity. The second easel was completely white and used only for showing finished canvases. The actual work was done on the table. It stood in front of the large window facing the rue du Départ, and was covered with a canvas waxed white and nailed to the underside of the boards . . . He had two large wicker armchairs, also painted white, and, on the scrupulously clean floor, two rugs, one red, the other grey. Such was the studio where Mondrian lived for thirteen years, where he received so many visitors, where he painted his most 'classical works,' the ones most justly admired, and where he also suffered a great deal from solitude, illness and poverty" (M. Seuphor, *Piet Mondrian*, p. 158).

One of Mondrian's contemporaries also attempted, somewhat later, to turn his studio into a work of art: the sculptor Constantin Brancusi. Brancusi, however, was primarily concerned with creating a space in which he could display his works to their best advantage, and then turned it into an environment, into a whole in which every sculpture was related to its neighbour and to the overall plan. Mondrian had an *a priori* conception of the studio as *a whole*

Poem, 1928
Lithography,
$25^3/8 \times 19^1/2$ in.
(64.3 × 49.5 cm)
Musée National d'Art
Moderne, Centre Georges
Pompidou, Paris

The Studio in Paris in 1926
Photo: Gemeentemuseum,
The Hague

in which to live. Far from being the most important thing in the studio, the painting on the easel was no more than an accessory, an element whose only *raison d'être* was to exist in relation to the overall equilibrium. Indeed, according to the "trialogue," it would be preferable for it to disappear: "If we organized our interiors along the lines of the New Plastic, the New Plastic paintings also could gradually disappear. As our complete 'Surroundings,' the New Plastic would be even more really alive" (*The New Art — The New Life*, p. 112). Easel painting was a prejudice from the past. But even Mondrian had to go on making easel paintings.

THE ARTIST AND HIS ERA

It would be a mistake to apply the image of the *artiste maudit* to Mondrian. His dignity and desire for order is hard to reconcile with the picturesque notion of an artistic bohemia. Whilst the poverty Seuphor mentions was real enough, the loneliness is debatable. Mondrian worked alone in the tranquillity of his studio, but he was neither a hermit nor a misanthrope. Ever since the days of the Hague school, he had always belonged to one or another group of artists. Even after the break with van Doesburg, he continued to be on good terms with several members of the *De Stijl* group, notably Vantongerloo and Oud. In the meantime, he became acquainted with Delmarle and the group centred on the journal *Vouloir* and with Seuphor, who founded a number of journals in which Mondrian could express himself freely. He later became a member of the Cercle et Carré (1930) and Abstraction-Création groups (1931–1936). He mixed with many artists, from Arp to Kandinsky and from Léger to Ben Nicholson. His personal fame extended to both the Bauhaus in Weimar and to the Circle group in England. Even though his work was never commercially successful, Mondrian was neither obscure nor lonely: in 1922 a retrospective to mark his fiftieth birthday was organized by the Stedelijk Museum in Amsterdam, the most famous museum in Holland.

Mondrian gradually fell out with van Doesburg from 1924 onwards when the latter began to paint his first *Counter-Compositions* (p. 31). These works are based upon the use of oblique lines, and thus break completely with neo-plasticism's horizontal-vertical rule. Mondrian disapproved of this deviation. But when *De Stijl*, which had been dormant in 1925, published van Doesburg's manifesto-essays on *elementarism* in 1926, Mondrian's irritation turned to anger. Neo-plasticism was relegated to the past in favour of a new art: "The construction method of elementarism is based upon the abolition of positive and negative by the *diagonal* and, in respect of colour, by the dissonant" (Jaffé, *De Stijl*, p. 214). The manifestoes contain many remarks which are philosophical rather than aesthetic, and they go completely against Mondrian's theories. Thus, "Elementarism preaches the total destruction of traditional absolutism in any form (the nonsense about a rigid opposition between man and woman, man and god, good and evil, etc.). The Elementarist sees life as a vast expanse in which these life factors are constantly alternating with one another" (ibid., p. 217). For Mondrian, this was aesthetic regression. He also saw the attack on "rigid oppositions" between man and woman and so on as an attack on himself. Cut to the quick, he immediately and haughtily replied in his article "Home-Street-City": "One cannot deny the naturalistic and capricious character of the oblique . . . This is where superficial attempts to find a new plastic expression lead: without desiring to, we return to nature" (*The New Art — The New Life*, p. 210). For Mondrian, who wanted to denaturalize, this was absolute nonsense. The break with *De Stijl* was final. Even before this break, there had in fact been friction between Mondrian and van Doesburg.

Mondrian was certainly impecunious, despite the modest help he received from a few friends and patrons. He could have tolerated the sacrifices he was making for the art of the future, were it not that he saw those around him returning to the old art. In the early 1920, a "return to order" was indeed taking place, and many artists who had, like Severini and Herbin, been members of the avant-garde were reverting to figurative painting. Mondrian refused to accept the aesthetic explanation for this, but he did accept the pragmatic explanation that they had to please buyers who were scarcely tempted by the new abstract art. In 1924, he therefore published an article in *De Stijl* on this critical period in the art market. He believed that it would not last, and denounced the *volte-face* of those who were deliberately allowing themselves to be "blown by the wind": "We do not protest the stagnation and retreat, which are but temporary and apparent. We do protest the *traiterous attitude of those who pioneered the new. We protest that many of them equate the new with the old*" (*The New Art — The New Life*, pp. 180–181). Mondrian obviously regarded van Doesburg's reintroduction of obliques into the plastic arts as a compromise and an act of treachery. Was van Doesburg already thinking of elementarism when he published Mondrian's article? Perhaps, but he certainly thought that Mondrian was making an unacceptable compromise when he turned to the question of the artist's means of subsistence, and argued that those who had the wherewithall to pay artists were rejecting them because they preferred naturalistic art. Mondrian argues that: "In spite of all, one can preserve the distinction between old and new in order to keep one's 'own art' pure. The artist has few chances to earn money outside his own field: if the buyers demand naturalistic art, then the artist can produce this with his skills, but *distinct* from his 'own work' " (ibid., p. 181). Acting on his own initiative, van Doesburg adds a footnote disassociating the journal from Mondrian: "The editors assume no responsibility for this statement." He was well aware that Mondrian had for years derived some of his income from painting naturalistic flowers in the style of those he had painted before the war. The flower paintings were sold for modest prices in Holland by a few friends. It was only in 1925 that Mondrian stopped painting them, probably because he was wounded by van Doesburg's disapproval. I do not think that there is any duplicity in Mondrian's attitude — a radical abstract artist who quietly paints watercolours of flowers to earn a living — but there is certainly a great ambiguity, and it was to pose a serious problem after his death.

Anecdotes about Mondrian's aversion for flowers and trees have been widely circulated and discussed. Seuphor, Arp, and Kandinsky report that he would ask to change places if he was sitting by a window from which he could

see trees. Then there was the single flower — an artificial flower painted completely white and captured on photograph — in the studio in the rue du Départ. This was presumably an ironic concession to femininity, as he disdainfully states in the "trialogue" that: "Naturalistic flowers are for children and the feminine spirit" (*The New Art — The New Life*, p. 118). We will have to return to this point, but before we do so, we have to recall the dozens and dozens of rustic landscapes Mondrian went on painting until 1908 . . . the magnificent dunes painted in 1910–1911 . . . the splendid studies of trees executed in 1912–1913 . . . and all the paintings, watercolours, and sketches of all kinds of flowers he made at various times: chrysanthemums, arums, lilies, amaryllis, sunflowers, gladioli, rhododendrons, marigolds, dahlias, and roses. All these flowers must stem from the pleasure of drawing and painting them, of studying their structures and colours. Given that Mondrian went on painting flowers after he had perfected his neo-plasticism, we have to conclude that, quite apart from the fact that there was a demand for them, it gave him more pleasure than painting windmills or people, even if they did represent a nature which was the antithesis of his "own art," to take up the distinction he made in 1924. Mondrian may well have claimed that he "preferred the Eiffel Tower to Mont Blanc," but he must have been secretly fascinated by flowers and nature, and must have had a love-hate relationship with the things that he evoked to define his art in negative terms. Be that as it may, Mondrian made a definite distinction between his pre–1910 flower paintings, which were part of this visual plastic, and the potboilers he executed later for commercial reasons. He did not recognize the latter as

being part of his *oeuvre* — and in that sense there is a great difference between Mondrian's position and that of the aging Giorgio de Chirico who, a few decades later, would produce copies of his early metaphysical works. The problem is that collectors have disregarded the artist's comments and have posthumously made these late flower paintings part of his *oeuvre*. This is not always for mercenary reasons but, quite apart from the fact that these undated works are easily confused, it may reflect the belief that everything an artist touches is art, though it seems Mondrian's wishes regarding his own work should be respected.

Mondrian's *oeuvre*, or his "own work" of the 1920s and 1930s is not concerned with trees and flowers but with arranging coloured lines and rectangles on a rectangular canvas. Far from being repetitive and monotonous, it definitely evolves and can be divided into clearly recognizable periods. Around 1925, for instance, Mondrian showed a greater willingness to work with a format he had already used in the past and which he would never completely abandon:

the square placed on its apex, or the diamond. Given that these works coincide with his quarrel with van Doesburg, Mondrian is no doubt insisting that only horizontal and vertical lines are acceptable and that the oblique edge of the canvas is not a line in the painting. The angled edge of the painting reinforces the verticals and horizontals: without losing their equilibrium, they extend beyond the space of the painting, as in *Diamond Painting in with Red, Yellow and Blue* (1921–1925, fig. 74) and *Composition I with Blue and Yellow* (1925, fig. 73). During the 1930s, the diamonds, like the other paintings, tend to become more stark, using few lines and little colour, and are all decentred to a greater or lesser extent as in *Foxtrot A* (1930, fig. 88), *Composition with Two Lines* (1931, fig. 90), *Composition with Yellow Lines* (1933, fig. 91).

The squares and rectangles are frontal, perfectly solid, and two-dimensional. Several painters of the same generation appear to have discovered this structure simultaneously. This more or less geometrical figure is, however, no more than a form, just like a face, or a horse. A portrait by Frans Hals and a portrait by Ingres, or a horse by Paolo Uccello and a horse by Franz Marc have no more in common than the various squares painted by Mondrian, Malevich, Klee, or Arp. Arp's squares (1916–1918) are collages assembled in accordance with "the laws of chance," and mingle freely in their space. The many squares painted by Paul Klee are also governed by whimsy. They form an irregularly painted grid, rather like a delicately patterned carpet; the whole canvas shimmers before our eyes, and seems to move or to belly out, as though it were reacting to some internal pressure. They make us smile or dream. All this is very different to Mondrian's deliberate order, precision, and stasis. Malevich's famous black and red squares (1915) are not perfectly square, but at best quadrangular. Their sides are not quite parallel and not orthogonal. Nor are they truly rectilinear. They are statements or questions, signs charged with meaning and obviously traced by a human hand (the issue is too complex to be discussed here, and the reader is referred to *Malévitch*, Paris: Cercle d'Art, 1991, pp. 124–131). They too are very different from Mondrian, whose squares and rectangles are self-referential, and not signs. Mondrian's paintings affect us by purely plastic means or, as he himself puts it, by

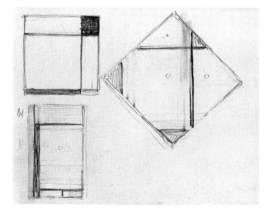

universal means: the tension of the perpendiculars, the equilibrium of the asymetrical parallelograms, and the relationship between the coloured and non-coloured surfaces. They are purely retinal, but they speak to the mind and the senses. Their beauty is very much their own.

In his first neo-plastic paintings, Mondrian used a lot of colour and a complex web of horizontals and verticals, but after 1922 it is noticeable that the drawing and, alternately, the colour becomes increasingly simplified. In the early 1930s, he was, as we have seen, content to use a single colour or non-colour (*Composition with Black Lines*, 1930; *Composition with Yellow Lines*, 1933), or two lines (*Composition with Two Lines*, 1931). No matter whether he uses one, two, or three colours, he always uses them sparingly: "A minimal colour area often suffices to produce equilibriated relationship with noncolour" (*The New Art — The New Life*, p. 197). More specifically, "*Equivalence* in the dimension and colour of the plastic means is necessary. Although varying in dimension and colour, the plastic means will nevertheless have an equal value. Generally, equilibrium implies a large area of noncolour or empty space opposed to a comparatively small area of colour or material" (ibid. p. 209). This principle governs all his paintings. The coloured surfaces are moved to the side (*Composition with Red, Yellow and Blue*, 1927; *Composition with White, Black and Red*, 1936, figs. 77, 98), or into the corners (*Composition with Red, Yellow and Blue*, 1928; *Composition with Red and Yellow*, 1937, figs. 84, 100). Symmetry is always avoided and the centre is never privileged. With some exceptions such as *Vertical Composition with Blue and White* (1936, fig. 95), Mondrian prefers to use more or less square canvases. He likes to give the impression that the painting is not square but rectangular by tracing skillfully decentred squares or by colouring one corner more than the other (*Composition with Red, Yellow and Blue*, 1928; *Composition*, 1929, figs. 84, 85). Sometimes a deliberate but discreet lack of symmetry seems to conceal a symmetry, as in the *Grey-Red Composition* of 1935 (fig. 92), with its decentred cross. In other paintings, the eye wanders across almost equal surfaces, as in the *Composition with Red and Blue* of 1936 (fig. 94).

When we come to the second half of the 1930s, there is a striking retreat from colour, and it coincides with the greater importance given to the horizontal and vertical lines, which now form a true grid. Still a light grid in 1936 (*Composition with Red and Blue*, *Composition with White, Black and Red*, figs. 94, 98), it becomes heavier and thicker in following years. In *Composition with Red and Yellow* (1937, fig. 100), *Composition with Blue* (1937, fig. 102) and even more so in *Composition 12 with Small Blue Square* (1936–1942, fig. 97), the black lines become bars — prison bars according to some commentators. And it is true that the threatening international climate of the late 1930s inevitably had its effects on the painter. When one looks closely at some of the paintings of this period, one finds that the black of the grid, which is glossier than the matt black of the painted rectangles, was applied last, as though the painting were locking up its colours behind the black grid.

THE STUDIO AND ITS PERSONA

Paradoxically, the artist who painted such serene works and whose writings are so positive and optimistic, was a man who was deeply disturbed by the violent turmoil of the world around him. The dictatorships and the increasingly real threats of war in the Western world worried Mondrian so much that in the autumn of 1938, he left Paris for London, which was further away from the Nazism, fascism, and Francoism on France's doorstep. But war soon broke out and his friends Naum Gabo, Ben Nicholson, and Barbara Hepworth sought refuge in Cornwall. When the first bombs began to fall near his studio, Mondrian was easily convinced by his friend Harry Holtzman's suggestion that he should go to the United States. He arrived there in October 1940, and at last felt safe and invigorated. A new stage in his work began.

The brief English period did not introduce any major changes into Mondrian's *œuvre*. The very small number of paintings he completed at this time show a greater emphasis on the black grid and the sparing use of colour already seen

New York City, Classical
Drawing No. 6, c 1941
Graphite on paper,
9×8¹/₄ in. (22.8×21 cm)

in previous years. In the *Composition with Red* of 1939 (fig. 104), the red occupies only a very small surface and leaves the white of the painting striped with black lines of varying thickness. During the early part of his stay in New York, Mondrian returned to some unfinished canvases (which is why they bear two dates). The black grids belong recognizably to the late 1930s. In some, the lines of the grid are still close together, as in *Composition with Red, Yellow and Blue*, (fig. 99) or in heavy black (*Composition with Red, Yellow and Blue*, 1936–1943, fig. 96), but the difference is that colour now tends to take up more of the surface. Although the colour is applied in flat rectangles, it sometimes escapes the framework previously provided by the black grid. This slight touch of fantasy marks a break with the austerity of the 1930s. Mondrian then completely abandons the austerity of old, as in *Place de la Concorde* (fig. 107). The canvas is dated 1939–1943 and, although it was begun in Paris, the colours indicate that it must have been completed during the New York period. In view of later developments, it should be noted that the areas of flat colour are now only slightly wider than the black lines. This is an important change in Mondrian's work, though it in no sense marks a departure from the principles of neo-plasticism. It was made possible by another, and perhaps more crucial, innovation made in 1941–1942.

New York City I (1942, fig. 109) is the work that signals the beginning of a new period. It is surprising because the black grid of previous years gives way to an irregular web of bands of primary colour which intersect freely (these grids are woven and not superimposed). The web is the colour's only support; there are no more flat areas of colour, and nor is there any black or grey colour (with the exception of the sober *Composition with Yellow Lines* of 1933). In this way, neo-plasticism was able to escape its serene, even austere, stasis and to use the dynamism of bright colour. Those who try to explain this sudden change, which occurred at the darkest moment of the war, invoke the effervescence of American life, which Mondrian found very attractive, and his joy at being safe at last and at achieving a certain success in artistic circles. It is, however, likely that he was again trying to breathe new life into the neo-plasticist formula. His working methods had also changed, as in addition to pencil and charcoal drawings, he was now making collages with coloured tape. The working drawings now looked more like the the finished paintings. In the few preparatory works that have survived we can see that initially Mondrian retained the black lines and the flat areas of colour between them. It was only in the final version that they were removed. It was his aesthetic evolution that gave rise to the new technique of making collages of coloured tape, and not vice versa.

Mondrian painted two other major works after *New York City*: *Broadway Boogie-Woogie* (1942–1943, fig. 111) and *Victory Boogie-Woogie* (1943–1944, fig. 112), which was left unfinished when he died. That Mondrian once entitled a painting *Fox-Trot* (1927) is an indication of his interest in that type of music or even dance, but it does not mean that we have to modify our interpretation of his work. The fact that Mondrian entitled the two works that mark the culmination of his career *Boogie-Woogie* does, however, mean that we have to look into something that is definitely neither a concession to fashion nor a whim.

Mondrian worked for a long time on these last paintings, which is why their complexity is more obvious than that of his starker canvases. Like *New York City I*, *Broadway Boogie-Woogie* uses no black, but grey is added to the three primary colours. Its structure is therefore more complicated: not only are some of the horizontal and vertical lines broken at the points where they intersect they are also divided into a sequence of small coloured rectangles. The spaces between them are either empty or occupied by

rectangular coloured surfaces —some surrounded by lines — and seven of those rectangles contain a further rectangle of a different
colour. That Mondrian was now leaving neo-
plasticist orthodoxy behind him is confirmed
by *Victory Boogie-Woogie*, where the white is no
longer the largest of all the coloured areas
that cover almost the whole canvas; the line of
small rectangles merge, and black reappears.
In other respects, it is difficult to evaluate this
work in progress, as some parts still have frag-
ments of paper pasted on to them. The lack of
precision in some of the painted planes indicate
that it is incomplete.

This dazzling use of colour by an artist who
had previously been so restrained is astonishing.
Critics have been too quick to see it as a reflection of New York. We should be wary of
the naturalistic transpositions that Mondrian
detested so much — the flickering coloured rectangles are no more the skyscrapers and neon
signs of Broadway than the rectangles of
previous decades were Dutch tiles or fields —
but there is no denying the impact, conscious
or otherwise, of the cultural and material environment. If we recall the interest in jazz that
Mondrian often expressed in his writings, it is
likely that the title supplies a more formal and
therefore more convincing explanation.

At the time when Mondrian reached New
York, boogie-woogie was very popular there.
This old form of piano blues had become
fashionable once more thanks to the successful
jazz concert given at Carnegie Hall by the
pianists Albert Ammons, Pete Johnson, and
Meade Lux Lewis in December 1938 (and jazz
in that temple to symphonic music was an event
in itself). Presumably because this music is less
melodic and more abruptly structured than
the jazz he had heard until then, Mondrian
developed a passion for it that surprises
historians. He was able to go to the Cafe Society, where Ammons and Johnson regularly played
duets, and he listened to the boogie-woogie
records of which he was so fond at home.
Boogie-woogie is a form of blues, usually taken
at a quick tempo, and is based on very dynamic
polyrhythms: while the left hand pounds a
repetitive and simple rhythmic figure — quaver-
semi-quaver-quaver in every bar — the right
hand plays a blues motif or hammers out short
phrases or riffs. Mondrian was clearly not at-
tempting to transpose this musical structure, but

one wonders if he did not see, after the event,
a visual equivalent in the horizontal-vertical
ostinato rhythm of his little rectangles, and the
coloured surfaces and the white silences that ac-
company them. The difference betwen *Broadway Boogie-Woogie* and *Victory Boogie-Woogie*
might be the difference between a boogie-
woogie solo and a duet or trio that saturates
the sonic space more thoroughly. As for the title's evocation of victory, it probably refers to
the victory of painting and neo-plasticism in particular rather than to the victory of the Allies,
which looked increasingly certain by late 1943.
As with other aspects of Mondrian's art, the
two explanations are not mutually exclusive.

Curiously enough, given that it meant a lot
to him, it was fairly late in life that for the first
time Mondrian unambiguously dealt with the
issue of how his paintings should be shown. In
an interview with James Johnson Sweeney in
1943, he discussed the frame, or rather the
absence of a frame, an important accessory
whose role in showing paintings had been
discussed for centuries by artists and collectors:
"So far as I know, I was the first to bring the
painting forward from the frame, rather than set
it within the frame. I had noted that a picture
without a frame works better than a framed
one and that the framing causes sensations of
three dimensions. It gives an illusion of depth,
so I took a frame of plain wood and mounted
my picture on it. In this way I brought to it a
more real existence" (*The New Art — The New
Life*, p. 357). Precisely when Mondrian made the
decision to show his paintings unframed is not
known, but he was probably not the first to do
so. Malevich, in particular, showed his paintings

without frames in the first suprematist exhibition of 1915 as a matter of principle.

We have seen that as well as painting and
writing, Mondrian always devoted time to the
plastic organization of his studio. Indeed, once
he found a space to his liking in New York,
he immediately began work on an installation
(the word had yet to become fashionable). The
studio (figs. 35, 36), which no longer exists, was
to have many imitators, and was described and
photographed by privileged witnesses like Harry
Holtzman: ''Although he lived there only five
months before he succumbed to pneumonia, he
worked with incredible concentration, energy,
and speed on its spatial organization, on the wall
compositions, and on the construction of the
desk and stool, worktable, shelf-cases and
tabouret. The *Wall Works 1943–1944* are the
only compositions he did on an environmental
scale, and the desk and stool and worktable are
his only three-dimensional constructions. The
studio, the evolution of which I witnessed
during my frequent visits, was Mondrian's last
work . . . The *Wall Works 1943–44* were com-
posed with rectangular cards of red, yellow,
blue, grey and white, tacked to the off-white
(*not white*) walls with small nails. The desk for
his bedroom-study was constructed from
segments of painting crates, the stool from an
apple box. The tabouret, and the shelves for

his paints, books, and papers, were made from
two-tiered orange crates tied together with
horizontal strips'' (*The New Art — The New Life*,
p. 5).

Many artists have intuitively seen their studios
as more or less consciously constructed
microcosms, which explains why there are so
many depictions of studios. Courbet even
painted his studio in order to expound his ideas
— though they were in truth social rather than
aesthetic. In the modern period, some artists
have turned their studios into carefully thought-
out spaces. The studios of Mondrian and Brancusi were the precursors of the installations that
were to proliferate a few decades later. As for
Kurt Schwitters, whose *Merz* construction
(*Merzsaüle*) gradually filled the studio and then
the floor above it, he stubbornly rebuilt his enormous contruction when, having been forced to
leave Hanover, he had to settle in Norway and
then England. Mondrian's studio has been
carefully studied ever since his intentions became
clear. It would, however, be a mistake to regard
his painting as secondary and to see the studio
as his *magnum opus*: to do would be to over-
systematize a system which is already very
systematic. Mondrian's approach was consistent
with his easel painting and everything else he did.
One wonders to what extent the artist became
part of his work by more or less consciously con-

structing a persona. A persona of this kind is neither a pose nor a fiction which takes control of its author (in the way that Jarry became the incarnation of his Ubu). The smiling Mondrian wore a tie as he worked to the sound of boogie-woogie in a meticulous *mise en scene* (pp. 10, 43). Yet he displayed none of the theatrical behaviour and persona of Yves Klein and Joseph Beuys. At the same time, and at the suggestion of the artist himself, certain details and certain events were blown out of all proportion by photographers and contemporary eye-witnesses, and then taken up with varying degrees of emphasis by the history of art. The studio in the rue du Départ was a calculated space in which nothing happened by chance (and no one understood this better than J. P. Raynaud, who used white tiles to emphasize the ''clinical'' aspect of his work) . . . and there was a flower in a vase in it. The conspicuous flower — and there was only one — was artificial, or in other words anti-natural. It was a human creation and what is more it was chromatically non-realistic, as it was painted completely white, or in other words purified of the green foliage the artist loathed, and of the capricious colours of stamens and corollas. The anecdotes about Mondrian's horror of nature, and especially his loathing for trees and flowers, have been repeated *ad nauseam*. Yet Mondrian's natural-artificial dichotomy was no more than a reaction against the constant talk of an eternal relationship between art and nature that he was forced to listen to. The artificial, colourless flower represents art's dominance over nature. The presence of this sign stresses the artificiality and artfulness of its environment. The persona of the artist who hates flowers must be, if not part of his work, at least in harmony with it. Later in his life, there were no discussions about the relationship between art and nature in New York. There was no need for an artificial flower in the studio on Fifty-ninth Street. Like the previous studio, it was designed to be a demonstration of principles as much as an exhibition. More than ever before, orthogonality was the absolute law that governed both the furniture and the walls, and the emptiness was underlined by the coloured rectangular mobiles. Entering this studio was, said Willem de Kooning, like ''walking around inside one of Mondrian's paintings'' (cited, *The New Art — The New Life*, p. 4).

At this point, it becomes necessary to make a digression. Lines at right-angles, a sparing use of colour, empty white spaces — anyone who is familiar with Korea or Japan cannot fail to be struck by the similarity between their traditional architecture and the way private houses are furnished, and neo-plasticist art, Mondrian's painting and the architecture of Rietveld (p. 38). A few studies do make the point in passing (notably Paul Overy in his *De Stijl*, London: Studio Vista, 1969) but they do not consider its implications. It is quite possible that this is a coincidence. The fact remains that between 1912 and 1913 van Doesburg did publish articles on Asiatic art and Japanese art in particular. In his monograph on van Doesburg, Joost Baljeu devotes precisely four lines to them and then moves on to a statement made by van Doesburg in a later article: ''What is happening is in fact a transition from an eastern notion of art to a western notion. It is possible that materialism has now destroyed itself'' (*''Le nouveau style en peinture''*, 1916). It is true that Mondrian scarcely mentions the art of the Far East in his writings, but that is not an adequate argument for refusing to discuss the topic. The architecture of Asia deserves at least as much attention as Madame Blavatsky's Asia.

Over-insistent spiritualist speculation tends to turn Mondrian into a ''literary'' artist. Mondrian was above all a plastician, and he was primarily concerned with the plastic. As he repeated on so many occasions, his ideas derived from his plastic work, and not vice versa.

The deliberately irregular stones of the walls of the Far East were cut at right angles and so arranged as to form a surface of rectangles of different sizes and an interplay of verticals and horizontals. This was for aesthetic rather than utilitarian reasons, whereas evenly calibrated stones or bricks are the usual motifs of western walls. There is some similarity between this oriental aesthetic and some Meso-American cycloppean buildings; but, ever since Antiquity, it has been very different to the ogives, round arches, rose windows, bull's eye windows, interlacing and arabesques, and all the other features we find in both the religious and secular architecture of the West, Islamic countries, and India or Indonesia. The perpendicular lines and simple forms of the architecture of the Far East are the deliberate mark of specifically human constructions, as opposed to the ambiant

a) Pulguksa temple wall, Kyongju, 8th century

b) Castle wall, Osaka, 16th century

c) Ninna-ji Temple, Kyoto (founded 886 A.D.)

d) *Pojagi*, Traditional Korean wrapping material, 19th century

e) Private house, Kyongju, Korea

a

b

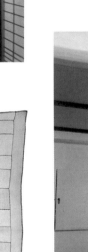

c

d

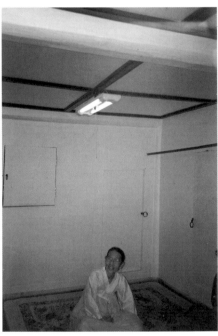

e

biomorphism of the rocks, pools, and streams, and the vegetation.

The same principle applies, on a different scale, to many objects in day to day use — fabrics, furniture, etc. There is the same attention to the balance between light and dark planes (light walls and dark openings, for instance) and the same distrust of oblique lines. The insistence on preserving right angles without introducing any sloping lines, and without altering the depth of the planes, thus explains the

preference given to sliding doors, as opposed to the hinged doors of the West.

Without going into more detail, we will simply note that the similarity with the work produced by *De Stijl* is obvious. We must stop arguing in terms of influence (a schoolmaster's concept: who copied whom?) and establish similarities or points of comparison; if we can do that, the discussion becomes interesting at the visual level, and then at the socio-cultural, philosophical, and other levels too.

THE NEO-PLASTICIST UTOPIA

Even in his old age, Mondrian constantly probed his art and its implications in his many writings. In 1941, he described it as a "non-subjective art," as opposed to the "non-objective art" proposed by Herbin, whom he criticised for referring to objects. In 1942–1943 he preferred to describe it as "a new realism" (see *The New Art — The New Life*, pp. 333–334, 345). His essential message is, however, contained in a book written mostly in 1931 and entitled *L'Art et la vie*. He went on revising, correcting and polishing it for years. Even at the height of the war in 1940, he was still hoping to publish it under the new titles *L'Art nouveau — La Vie nouvelle*. His hopes came to nothing. The book appeared posthumously in English. Many commentators (eg. Harry Holtzman and Herbert Henkels) therefore regard it as his testament, and rightly so.

Ever since he discovered the principles of neo-plasticism, Mondrian had insisted that art is not a decorative element to be added to the environment or to be exhibited — a painting on a wall, a statue in a room in a museum — but an integral part of the urban environment. To that extent, he was fully in agreement with his friend Fernand Léger, whose every effort was devoted to making art part of the city (see Fauchereau, *Fernand Léger: A Painter in the City*, New York: Rizzoli 1994). Mondrian began to transpose the principles of neo-plasticist painting to architecture and then town-planning in his 1919 "trialogue," but with *L'Art nouveau-La Vie Nouvelle*, he attempts to go further still and to extend them to the fabric of society. Ever since the days when he had painted works of political and religious propaganda for his father, Mondrian had always taken an interest in society. The tendency to expand the domain of art, which is apparent in his very first contributions to *De Stijl*, became more and more pronounced with *L'Art nouveau-La Vie Nouvelle*.

As always, Mondrian defines art as the human, as opposed to nature. Neo-plasticism radically rejects nature in the name of progress. "The more human progress asserts itself, the more violently does natural instinct fight against it. For progress involves *diminishing the privileges of the natural state*" (*The New Art — The New Life*, pp. 264–265). When Kandinsky or Arp describe how Mondrian would protest at the very sight of a tree, one smiles, just as one smiles at his joke about preferring the Eiffel Tower to Mont Blanc, but when he attempts to reduce nature as a matter of principle, as he stresses here, we tend to bridle because we live in an era which ecology has sensitized to the threats posed by over-zealous architects, no matter how "artistic" they may be. Like the futurists before him, Mondrian had a boundless faith in progress. Far from disturbing him, the cult of the machine and rampant urbanization seemed to him to provide the key to happiness. Whilst he may not speak of harmony in the way that the utopian Robert Owen does he does speak as an artist, of equilibrium and universality, and looks to the future with confidence: "Let us see what exclusive concentration upon utility and practical life will produce. The future will establish true beauty and true life — and in a new form," (ibid., p. 264). But he also insisted that "human" was the opposite of "individual." Mondrian thought that the old attitude of the artist, concerned only with his ego and with imposing his own personality, was at work in society as a whole. He also thought that individualism was the source of all evils: nationalism, militarism, and egotism in general. We are very close here to the arguments put forward by Georges Sorel in his famous essay on "the social value of art." Whereas "Every cultural element must be universalized," writes Sorel, "every artist shuts himself up in his studio, and devotes all his efforts to perfecting his own technique, so as to demonstrate his skill in his speciality" ("La Valeur sociale de l'art," *Revue de Métaphysique et de morale*, vol. 9, 1901). The parallel should not be taken too far, as Sorel's artistic tastes were far too conservative to appeal to a member of the avant-guard. The fact remains, however, that any intellectual working in the early twentieth century inevitably knew something about the theories of Sorel, whose fame was based upon his *Reflections sur la violence* (1908).

For Mondrian, the "human" meant solidarity in the face of all forms of individualism, the quest for aesthetic originality, usury and the arms industry, or in short "all speculators and exploiters." Pursuing the same argument, he transposes the vocabulary of neo-plasticism and proposes to "create pure relationships. *The* essential value of each individual entitles him to an existence equivalent to that of others; if disabled, he must be supported in keeping with the value that he is unable to realize: he is a communal responsibility" (*The New Art — The New Life*, p. 267). Human solidarity is an equivalent to the aesthetic of Mondrian's paintings. Look at them and tranpose them: a small blue rectangle has little value in itself, but when it is juxtaposed with a large yellow rectangle, an equivalence is created and a balanced whole is created. Relations of equivalence and relations of equality. Neo-plasticism teaches a "new morality" (and, as described by Mondrian, it is not dissimilar to the "higher production" of the universal society of the future, which, according to *Reflections sur la violence*, is prefigured by art). As Mondrian puts it: "High universal morality finds its expression in the apogee of the culture of equivalent relationships. Art in its end demonstrates that only line and colour free from all oppression of form can constitute equivalent relationships. Thus in life only the free individual and groups of free individuals can form a mutually equivalent organization and become capable of realizing the content of high universal morality, which prescribes what we live for each and for all" (ibid., p. 270). Mondrian was not one of those who believe that man is fundamentally good, but always perverted by society. His unshakeable optimism, and his faith in the fundamental goodness of men who are capable or organizing themselves into a fair society, both stem from his art: "The day will come when the individual will be capable of governing himself. The new art demonstrates all this. In opposition to the art of the past, where particular forms dominate one another, the neutral and universal forms of the new art do not assert themselves at one another's expense" (ibid., pp. 265–266). In a crucial and inspired passage, he describes what the world will be like when it conforms to neo-plasticist values; it has lost none of its power for anyone who is willing to meditate upon it:

"In life, reorganization must not be limited to individual forms, each for its own sake, but must be extended universally throughout life.

"In politics, it is not enough to work toward internally equivalent relationships, we must above all achieve equivalent relationships of international order.

"In art, Neo-Plastic demonstrates this necessity most exactly. Through intersecting lines, the mutual relationships destroy each plane's separateness so that all unite completely.

"The rectangular planes of varying dimensions and colours visibly demonstrate that *internationalism* does not mean chaos ruled by monotony but an ordered and clearly divided unity. In Neo-Plastic there are, in fact, very definite boundaries. But these boundaries are not really closed; the straight lines in rectangular opposition constantly intersect, so that their rhythm continues throughout the whole work. In the same way, in the international order of the future the different countries, while being mutually equivalent, will have their unique and different value. There will be just frontiers, proportionate to the value of each country in relationship to the whole federation. These frontiers will be clearly defined but not 'closed'; there will be no customs, no work permits. 'Foreigners' will not be viewed as aliens. . .

"If art demonstrates that the mutual separation of forms increases their intrinsic value and produces a more perfect union, we can also note with satisfaction the separation of church and state, the separation of religion from learning or philosophy. Liberated and restored to independence, everything more easily achieves profundity.

"All the old limiting forms, like family, country, etc., long cultivated and protected by church and state and still necessary today, are seen by the new mentality, in their conventional sense, as obstacles to truly human life. In their present form they oppose the establishment of pure social relationships and individual liberty . . .

"Just as art has slowly created a new plastic expression of more real equilibrium, life itself will slowly create this equilibrium in a new social and economic organization" (*The New Art — The New Life*, pp. 268–269). The "new morality" will provide the basis for a universal equilibrium, and it will eventually reshape relations between men and women, and all human relations. There will be no more marriage, no more family and no more countries in the sense in which we now understand those terms. According to Mondrian, religions will be replaced by the universal and sacred element in art. The latter term is to be understood as meaning *art in life*, as Mondrian had long ago announced the end of art, as practised today — and even the end of art as he practised it, given that he could go no further and still be understood and accepted. At the same time, he took the view that art is "an oppression" because it " 'replaces' true life as an abstract domain" (ibid., p. 336). Yet Mondrian was confident that art would become an integral part of life: all his faculties and all his experience told him so:

"Intuition makes us feel what is right. Reason realizes, finds out the laws.

"The new religion without churches is the old religion *free of all oppression*.

"The new art is the old art *free of all oppression*.

"Modern buildings which evoke the sense of beauty replace churches.

"In this way art becomes religion.

"The new religion is faith in life" (ibid., p. 319).

This is pure utopianism. And yet the man who is speaking here claims not to be dreaming; like his compatriot Multatuli, he is a basically generous preacher. From this point onwards, he is not speculating, but making assertions.

Taken as a whole, the originality of Mondrian's utopia is very relative. The conviction that the golden age lies ahead of us and not behind us, and the hopes placed in technology and industry can already be found in Saint-Simon. The need for "universal unity" can be found in Fourier, and the attacks on the family, religion patriotism and national frontiers can be found in Owen, who foresaw villages built in the shape of parallelograms. The great difference between Mondrian and the utopians of the nineteenth century is that he begins with a practice and then a theory of art which he extends to men and the world. A comparison of Mondrian's ideas and their social utopias is not, however, devoid of interest if we concentrate on similarities and not a mere search for hypothetical influences. I can only add that, given the modest dimensions of this study, it is not really possible to raise the issue of the similarity between the neo-plasticist utopia and the many proposals put forward at the turn of the century by theorists who had anarchist leanings. To do so would add a further dimension to Mondrian's thought. There has been so much talk about Mondrian and Blavatsky, Schoenmakers, and theosophy, that we tend to forget that Kropotkin, Tolstoy, Sorel, and Elysée Reclus were also widely discussed at this time. Kandinsky and Kupka often refer to them. Why should Mondrian have been less well-informed? Whereas Kandinsky and Kupka concentrate solely on the aesthetic in their writings, it is important to remember Mondrian's boldness, as he wanted in principle to go beyond art, to make art merge into life. From that point of view, only Malevich can really be compared with him.

Given that he was a plastic artist, it was ultimately only natural that his attempt to restructure the world by establishing new values and new relationships that would create a truly universal equilibrium should begin with a discussion of the question of space. Mondrian extended the new spatial organization of his paintings to his own personal space — his studio. He would have liked to extend it to the entire world. It is probably preferable for it to remain autopia, as it has to be admitted that intransigent artists like Mondrian and Malevich are so sure of being right that they sometimes fail to take into consideration anything that stands in their way. Too bad for anyone who prefers Mont Blanc to the Eiffel Tower or trees that grow freely to concrete buildings, even if they are neoplasticist. Too bad for those for whom the human and the natural (flowers!) are not opposites. Half-measures are not to the liking of true reformers. The most beautiful thing about utopias is, perhaps, the fact that they remain utopias.

Moralists claim that men should be judged by what they do and not by what they say. That is quite possible. Yet Mondrian's discourse, which is so strict and so magnificently lacking in moderation, teaches us to look more closely at his paintings. It teaches us to see in them a generosity which is not apparent at first sight, and, perhaps, to see something else. Look at Mondrian's paintings. Of course they are beautiful, but they also contain a message of optimism and serenity.

CHRONOLOGY

Mondrian, 1899

Mondrian, c 1907

1872
Pieter Cornelis Mondriaan is born into a strict Calvinist family living near Utrecht. His father, a headmaster, is a strong supporter of the religious and social ideas of the Dutch Reformed Party. In 1880, the family moves to Winterwijk, where his father has been appointed to a new post.

1889
Mondrian, who began to paint and to assist his father with commissions for historical and social prints at a very early age, obtains a diploma qualifying him to teach drawing in primary schools. His uncle, the painter Frits Mondriaan, is generous with his advice.

1892
Obtains a second diploma qualifying him to teach in secondary schools, but decides to devote himself to the fine arts, much to the disappointment of his family. A grant allows him to attend courses at the Amsterdam Academy. Becomes friends with the old painter Braet von Uberfeldt, who lends him documents on art history.

1893
Supports himself by making copies in the Rijkmuseum, painting portraits and landscapes, and giving private lessons. Exhibits with local associations.

1898
Unsuccessful in Prix de Rome competition. He will enter again in 1901, once more without success.

1899
Period of crisis, during which he thinks momentarily of becoming a preacher. Meets Albert van den Briel, a student who will remain his friend. They study theosophy together.

1900
Paints landscapes on the banks of the Gein and in the area around Amsterdam until 1903.

1901
Visits Spain with the painter Simon Maris; the trip has no impact on his work. Meets Jan Sluyters.

1903
A visit to Brabant fills him with enthusiam; he returns there and lives in Uden from January 1904 to January 1905.

1905
Returns to Amsterdam. Van Gogh retrospective at the Stedelijk Museum.

1907
Summer in Oele. Paints nocturnal landscapes. Sees Van Dongen's fauvist paintings.

1908
First visit to Domburg in Zeeland, the home of Jan Toorop and a small community of artists. His palette lightens under the influence of divisionism.

1909.
Exhibits with Sluyters and Cornelis Spoor at the Stedlijk Museum. His expressionist-style works are severely criticised. Joins the Dutch Theosophical Society. More visits to Domburg.

1910
Together with Conrad Kickert and Sluyters, he is one of the founders of the Moderne Kunstring, which was established to promote avant-garde art. Takes part in an exibition by the luminists.

1911
The Moderne Kunstring organizes an exhibition including Picasso, Braque, Derain, Le Fauconnier and others. Executes *Evolution*, a "theosophical painting." Decides to leave for Paris, the centre of the new painting.

1912
In Paris, he visits Fernand Léger and especially Dutch artists like Van Dongen, L. Schelfhout, O. van Rees, Jacoba van Heemskerck and the composer Jacob van Domselaer. Begins to spell his name *Mondrian* and adopts cubism. Exhibits with the Independents in Paris, as well as in Holland and Germany.

1913
Continues his cubist experiments. Diego Rivera and Lodewijk Schelfhout are his neighbours at 26 rue du Départ.

1914
First one-man show in The Hague. War breaks out while he is in Holland, and he is unable to return to Paris until the end of the war. Returns to Domburg and makes more studies of the sea and of church facades.

1915
Works in Laren, together with his friend Jacob van Domselaer. Meets the esoteric philosopher M. H. J. Schoenmaekers and regularly visits the Slijpers, who become his most important collectors. First contacts with Theo van Doesburg.

1916
Meets Bart van der Leck, whose flat paintings interest him. Van der Leck comes to live in Laren.

1917
First compositions using coloured rectangles. Van Doesburg publishes the first issue of *De Stijl*. The journal begins to publish his essay "The New Plastic in Painting."

1918
First diamond-shaped compositions.

1919
Returns to Paris and to his old studio in the rue du Départ. Apart from the period 1920–1921, when he occupies a studio in the rue de Coulmiers, he will remain there until 1935. *De Stijl* publishes his "trialogue" "Natural Reality and Abstract Reality." Arranges his studio in accordance with these principles.

1920

Galerie Léonce Rosenberg publishes his pamphlet *Le Néo-Plasticisme* in French. Meets the sculptor Georges Vantongerloo.

1921

Defends the Italian *bruiteurs* in an article on music. Beginning of a difficult period; naturalistic paintings of flowers help him to survive.

1922

Retrospective exhibition at the Stedelijk Musuem in Amsterdam to mark his fiftieth birthday.

1923

Begins to use only three primary colours and three non-colours. Meets Michel Seuphor.

1924

Last article in *De Stijl*; disapproves of the *elementarism* promoted by van Doesburg. The friction between the two will increase until the final break in 1927.

1925

The Bauhaus publishes a selection of his *De Stijl* articles under the title *Neue Gestaltung*. Mondrian now enjoys growing fame in both Europe and America, and his work is frequently exhibited.

1926

Maquettes for *Salon de Mme. B. à Dresde* and *L'Éphémère est éternel*, a play by Seuphor.

1930

Joins the Cercle et Carré group founded by Seuphor and Torres-Garcia.

1931

Joins the Abstraction-Création group founded by Vantongerloo and Auguste Herbin. Reconciliation with Van Doesburg shortly before the latter's death. Writes a first draft of *L'Art et la vie*, which will subsequently become *L'Art nouveau — La Vie nouvelle* and finally *The New Art — The New Life*.

1934

Makes the acquaintance of Ben Nicholson and Barbara Hepworth, and then Harry Holtzman.

1935

The compulsory purchase of 26 rue du Départ for demolition forces him to move to less comfortable surroundings at 278 boulevard Raspail.

1938

The Munich Agreement and the Spanish Civil War fill him with terror. In the autumn, he leaves for London, where he lives near the Nicholsons in Hampstead.

1940

London is bombed. In October, he leaves for New York, where Holtzman and Fritz Glarner are expecting him. His studio is at 353 East 56th Street.

1941

New York City: coloured lines replace black lines.

1942

Broadway Boogie-Woogie: the coloured lines are broken. First one-man show in New York at the Valentine Dudensing Gallery.

1943

Second one-man show. Begins *Victory Boogie-Woogie*. On 1 October, he moves to a new studio at 15 East 59th Street and begins to decorate it in accordance with neo-plasticist principles.

1944

Dies of pneumonia on 1 February. His friends Holtzman and Glarner open the studio for six weeks before dismantling it. Mondrian is buried in Cypress Hill Cemetery, Brooklyn.

1945

Posthumous retrospective at Museum of Modern Art, New York. To mark the occasion a collection of texts edited by Holtzman is published under the title *Plastic Art and Pure Plastic Art*.

Mondrian, Enrico Prampolini, and Michel Seuphor, 1926

Mondrian in his studio on First Avenue, 1942 (Photograph: Arnold Newman)

CONCISE BIBLIOGRAPHY

The present study is based primarily on Mondrian's writings. A good complete edition has been produced by Harry Holtzman and Martin S. James: *The New Art — The New Life: The Collected Writings of Piet Mondrian*, London: Thames and Hudson, 1987. Reference has also been made to a number of catalogues raisonnés, which sometimes give conflicting information:

Michel Seuphor, *Piet Mondrian*: Life and Work, London: Thames and Hudson, 1957. (This is an essential work of reference.)

Maria Grazia Ottolenghi, *L'Opera completa di Mondrian*, Milan: Rizzoli, 1974.

Cor Blok, *Mondrian: een catalogue von zijn werk in Nederlands openbaar bezit*, Amsterdam: Meulenhoff, 1974.

The following have also been consulted:

H. L. C. Jaffé, *Piet Mondrian*, Paris: Cercle d'Art, 1970, 1991.

Robert Welsh, *The Early Career of Piet Mondrian*, New York: Garland, 1977.

Charles de Mooij and Meureen Trappeniers, *Piet Mondrian: Een jaar in Brabant, 1904–1905*, Waanders: Zwolle, 1991.

The full Mondrian bibliography is immense and there are numerous exhibition catalogues. Because of the quality of the texts (by H. Henkels, H. Holtzman, R. Welsh, J. Joosten, and K. von Maur) mention should be made of the catalogue to the exhibition shown in Stuttgart, The Hague, and Baltimore (6 December 1980–20 December 1981), now included in *L'Atelier de Mondrian* (Paris: Macula, 1982) and in the catalogue to the Toky Shimbun exhibition *Mondrian from Figuration to Abstraction*, London: Thames and Hudson, 1987. Herbert Henkel's text is also reprinted in the catalogue to the Fondation Maeght exhibition (Saint-Paul, 1985).

ILLUSTRATIONS

1
Woods and Stream, 1888
Charcoal and chalk,
24³/₄ × 18⁷/₈ in. (62 × 48 cm)
Gemeentemuseum,
The Hague

2
Young Girl Writing, c. 1890
Black chalk,
22¹/₂ × 17¹/₂ in. (57 × 44.5 cm)
Gemeentemuseum,
The Hague

3

3
Lonely House, 1898–1900
Watercolour and gouache,
17$^7/_8$×23 in. (45.5×58.5 cm)
Gemeentemuseum,
The Hague

4

5

4
Woods, 1898–1900
(or earlier)
Watercolour and gouache
on paper,
17⁷/₈×22¹/₂ in. (45.5×57 cm)
Gemeentemuseum,
The Hague

5
Boat on the Amstel: Evening,
1900–1902
Watercolour and pencil,
21⁵/₈×26 in. (55×66 cm)
Gemeentemuseum,
The Hague

6

6
Young Girl, 1900–1901
(or later)
Oil on canvas,
$20^7/_8 \times 17^3/_8$ in. (53 × 44 cm)
Gemeentemuseum,
The Hague

7

8

7
Farm, 1902–1904
Watercolour,
20 1/8 × 25 3/4 in. (51 × 65.5 cm)
Gemeentemuseum,
The Hague

8
Mill by the Water, c. 1905
Oil on canvas mounted on
cardboard,
11 7/8 × 15 in. (30.2 × 38.1 cm)
Collection of The Museum
of Modern Art, New York,
Purchase Photograph © (1994)
The Museum of Modern Art,
New York

9

10

9
Sheepfold at evening, 1906
Charcoal, pencil and
watercolour,
29 1/8 × 38 5/8 in. (74 × 98 cm)
Gemeentemuseum,
The Hague

10
Farm at Nistelrode,
1904–1905
Watercolour,
17 1/2 × 24 3/4 in. (44.5 × 63 cm)
Gemeentemuseum,
The Hague

11

12

13

14

11
*Banks of the Gein by
Moonlight*, 1907–1908
Oil on canvas,
31 1/8×36 3/8 in. (79×92.5 cm)
Gemeentemuseum,
The Hague

12
Evening over the Gein,
1906–1907
Oil on canvas,
25 5/8×33 7/8 in. (65×86 cm)
Gemeentemuseum,
The Hague

13
Windmill at evening, c 1907
Charcoal,
41 3/8×35 1/2 in. (105×90 cm)
Gemeentemuseum,
The Hague

14
The Windmill, 1907–1908
Oil on canvas,
39 3/8×37 1/4 in.
(100×94.5 cm)
Stedelijk Museum,
Amsterdam

15

15
Landscape with Red Cloud,
1907
Oil on card,
25 $^1/_4$×29 $^1/_2$ in. (64×75 cm)
Gemeentemuseum,
The Hague

16
Landscape, 1907
Oil on card,
25 $^1/_4$×30 $^1/_8$ in. (64×76.5 cm)
Gemeentemuseum,
The Hague

16

17

18

17
Windmill at evening, 1908
Oil on canvas,
40 1/2 × 33 7/8 in. (103 × 86 cm)
Gemeentemuseum,
The Hague

18
Windmill by Sunlight, 1908
Oil on canvas,
44 7/8 × 34 1/4 in. (114 × 87 cm)
Gemeentemuseum,
The Hague

19

20

21

19
The Blue Tree, 1908
Tempera on card,
29³/₄×39¹/₈ in.
(75.5×99.5 cm)
Gemeentemuseum,
The Hague

20
The Red Tree, 1908
Oil on canvas,
27⁵/₈×39 in. (70×99 cm)
Gemeentemuseum,
The Hague

21
Wood near Oele, 1908
Oil on canvas,
11×62¹/₄ in. (128×158 cm)
Gemeentemuseum,
The Hague

22

22
Rhododendrons, 1909–1910
Charcoal and pastel on beige paper,
28³/₄×38³/₈ in. (73×97.5 cm)
Gemeentemuseum,
The Hague

23
Sunflower II, 1907–1908
Oil on card,
25⁵/₈×13³/₈ in. (65×34 cm)
Gemeentemuseum,
The Hague

24
Chrysanthemum, 1909
Gouache,
27¹/₈×10³/₄ in. (69×26.5 cm)
Gemeentemuseum,
The Hague

25
The Tree, c. 1908
Oil on canvas,
42⁷/₈×28¹/₂ in.
(109.2×72.4 cm)
McNay Art Museum,
San Antonio, Texas
Gift of Alice Hanszen

23

24

26

27

26
Dune II, 1909–1910
Oil on canvas,
15×18 1/4 in. (38×46.5 cm)
Gemeentemuseum,
The Hague

27
Dune IV, 1909–1910
Oil on canvas,
13×18 1/8 in. (33×46 cm)
Gemeentemuseum,
The Hague

28
Zeeland Farmer, 1909–1910
Oil on canvas,
27 1/8×20 7/8 in. (69×53 cm)
Gemeentemuseum,
The Hague

28

29

30

29
Lighthouse near Westkapelle,
1909–1910
Oil on canvas,
53 1/8 × 29 1/2 in. (135 × 75 cm)
Gemeentemuseum,
The Hague

30
Lighthouse near Westkapelle,
1908–1909
Ink, pencil and gouache,
11 7/8 × 9 5/8 in. (30 × 24.5 cm)
Gemeentemuseum,
The Hague

31
Passion Flower, 1908–1909
Watercolour,
28 1/2 × 18 1/4 in.
(72.5 × 46.5 cm)
Gemeentemuseum,
The Hague

PASSIE BLOEM.   PIET MONDRIAAN.

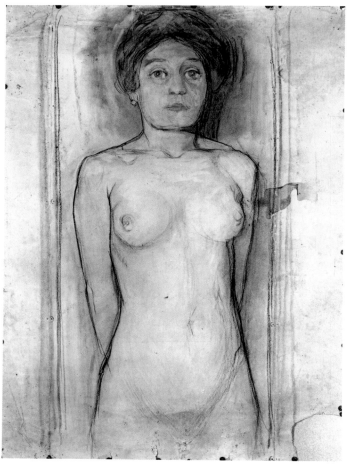

32

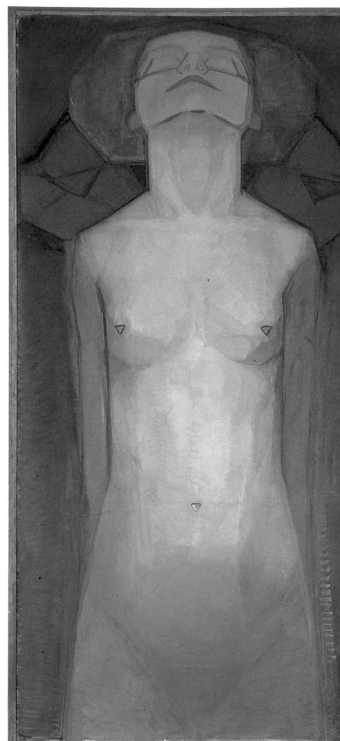

32
Nude, 1908–1911
Black chalk,
33 7/8 × 16 1/2 in. (86×42 cm)
Gemeentemuseum,
The Hague

33
Evolution, 1910–1911
Oil on canvas, triptych,
70 1/8×33 1/2 in., 72×34 1/2 in.,
70 1/2×33 1/2 in.
(178×85 cm, 183×87.5 cm,
178×85 cm)
Gemeentemuseum,
The Hague

33

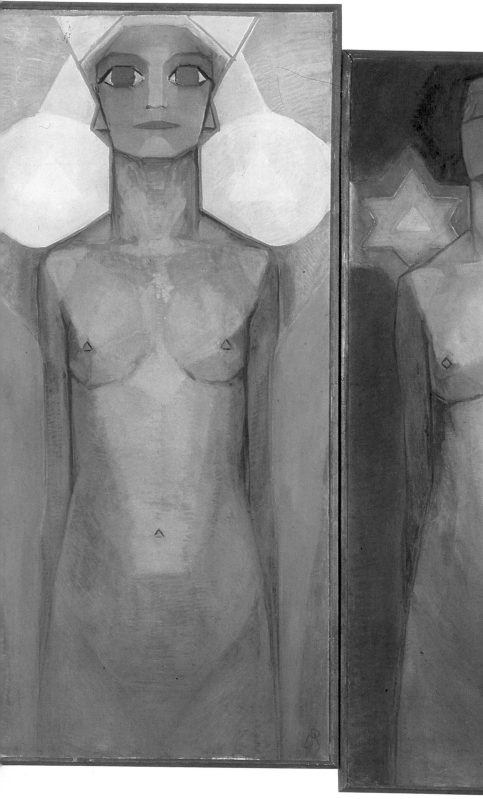
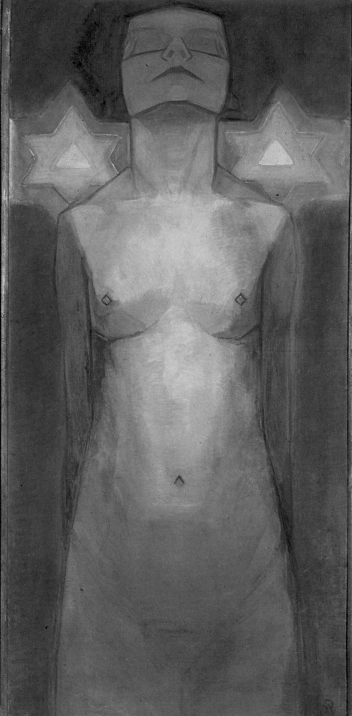

34

35

36

34
Church in Domburg,
1910–1911
Oil on canvas,
44⁷/₈×29¹/₂ in. (114×75 cm)
Gemeentemuseum,
The Hague

35
Landscape: Dunes, c 1911
Oil on canvas,
55¹/₂×94¹/₈ in. (141×239 cm)
Gemeentemuseum,
The Hague

36
The Red Mill, 1911
Oil on canvas,
9×33⁷/₈ in. (150×86 cm)
Gemeentemuseum,
The Hague

37

38

39

37
Still Life with Ginger Pot I,
1911–1912
Oil on canvas,
5 3/4 × 29 1/2 in. (65.5 × 75 cm)
Gemeentemuseum,
The Hague

38
Nude, 1912
Oil on canvas,
55 1/8 × 38 5/8 in. (140 × 98 cm)
Gemeentemuseum,
The Hague

39
Still Life with Ginger Pot II,
1912
Oil on canvas,
36 × 47 1/4 in. (91.5 × 120 cm)
Gemeentemuseum,
The Hague

40

40
Landscape with Trees, 1912
Oil on canvas,
47 1/4 × 39 3/8 in. (120 × 100 cm)
Gemeentemuseum,
The Hague

41

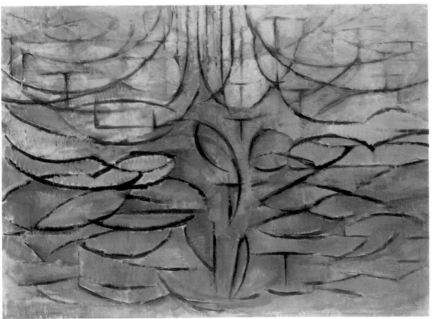

42

41
Tree, c. 1912
Oil on canvas,
37×27⅞ in. (94×70.8 cm)
Carnegie Institute, Museum
of Art, Pittsburgh

42
Apple Tree in Blossom, 1912
Oil on canvas,
30¾×41¾ in. (78×106 cm)
Gemeentemuseum,
The Hague

43

43
Composition: Trees II,
1912–1913
Oil on canvas,
38 5/8 × 25 5/8 in. (98 × 65 cm)
Gemeentemuseum,
The Hague

44
*Composition of Lines and
Colours,* 1913
Oil on canvas,
25 1/4 × 37 in. (64.1 × 94 cm)
Rijksmuseum Kröller-Müller,
Otterlo

44

45

45
Composition VII, 1913
Oil on canvas,
41 1/8×44 3/4 in.
(104.4×113.6 cm)
The Solomon
R. Guggenheim Foundation,
New York
Photograph: David Heald,
© The Solomon
R. Guggenheim Foundation,
New York

46

46
*Composition of Lines and
Colours (Windmill)*, 1913
Oil on canvas,
45 1/4×34 5/8 in. (115×88 cm)
Rijksmuseum Kröller-Müller,
Otterlo

47
Oval Composition III, 1914
Oil on canvas,
55 1/8×39 3/4 in. (140×101 cm)
Stedelijk Museum,
Amsterdam

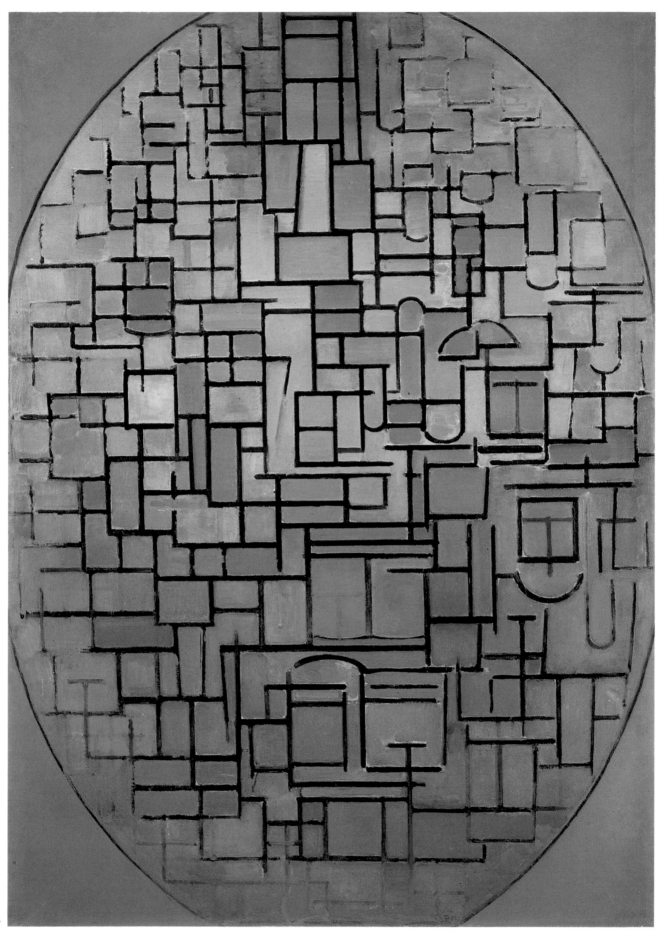

48

48
Oval Composition (Trees),
1913
Oil on canvas,
37×29⁷/₈ in. (94×76 cm)
Stedelijk Musuem,
Amsterdam

49
Colour Planes in an Oval,
1913–1914
Oil on canvas,
42³/₈×31 in. (107.6×78.8 cm)
Collection of the Museum of
Modern Art, New York
(Acquisition)
Photograph © (1993) The
Museum of Modern Art,
New York

50
Composition in an Oval: KUB,
1914
Oil on canvas,
44¹/₂×33¹/₄ in.
(113×84.5 cm)
Gemeentemuseum,
The Hague

49

51

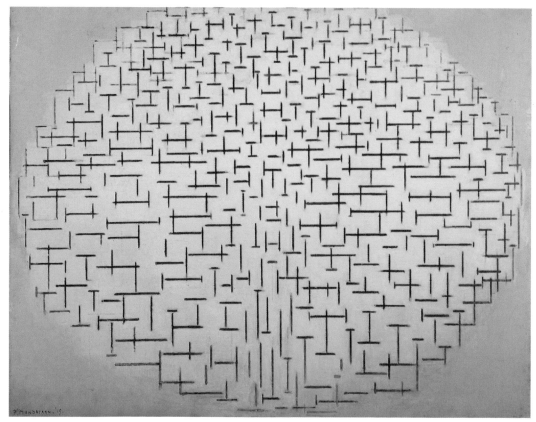

52

51
Farm at Duivendrecht,
1915–1916 (or 1906–1908)
Oil on canvas,
33 5/8 × 42 3/4 in.
(85.5 × 108.5 cm)
Gemeentemuseum,
The Hague

52
Composition No. 10, 1915
Oil on canvas,
33 1/2 × 42 1/2 in. (85 × 108 cm)
Rijksmuseum Kröller-Müller,
Otterlo

53

53
Self-Portrait, 1918
Oil on canvas,
34⅝×28 in. (88×71 cm)
Gemeentemuseum,
The Hague

54

54
*Composition with Colour
Planes A*, 1917
Oil on canvas,
19 3/4 × 17 3/8 in. (50 × 44 cm)
Rijksmuseum Kröller-Müller,
Otterlo

55

55
*Composition with Colour
Planes No. 3,* 1917
Oil on canvas,
18⁷/₈×24 in. (48×61 cm)
Gemeentemuseum,
The Hague

56

56
*Composition in Black and
White*, 1917
Oil on canvas,
42 1/2 × 42 1/2 in. (108 × 108 cm)
Rijksmuseum Kröller-Müller,
Otterlo

57
Composition, 1916
Oil on canvas,
46 7/8 × 29 1/2 in.
(119 × 75.1 cm)
The Solomon
R. Guggenheim Foundation,
New York
Photograph: David Heald,
© The Solomon
R. Guggenheim Foundation,
New York

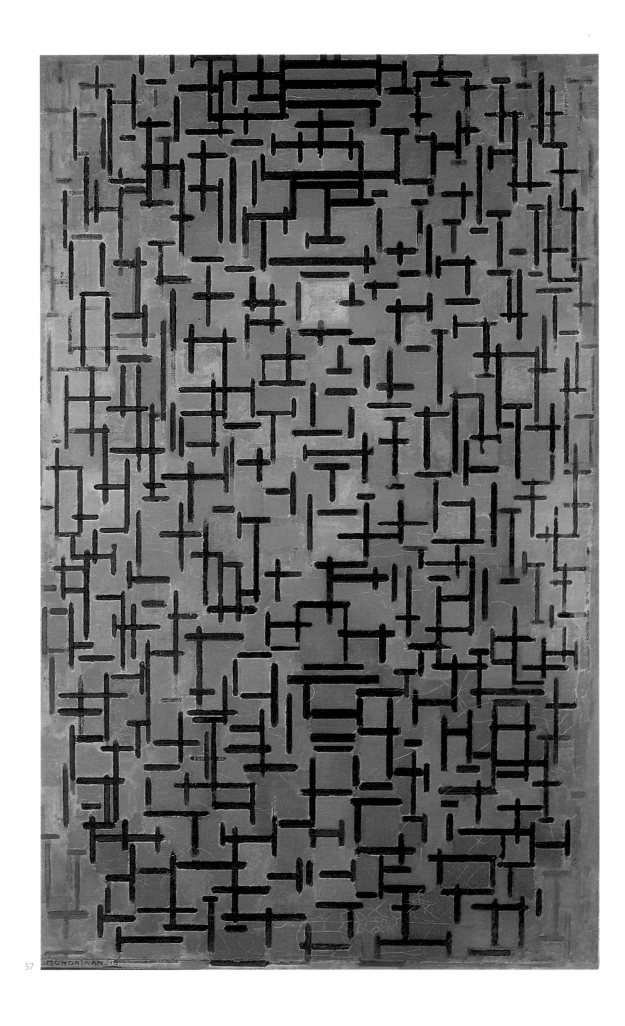

58

58
*Composition in Diamond
Shape*, 1918–1919
Oil on canvas,
diag. 26 ¹/₄ in. (67 cm)
Rijksemusem Kröller-Müller,
Otterlo

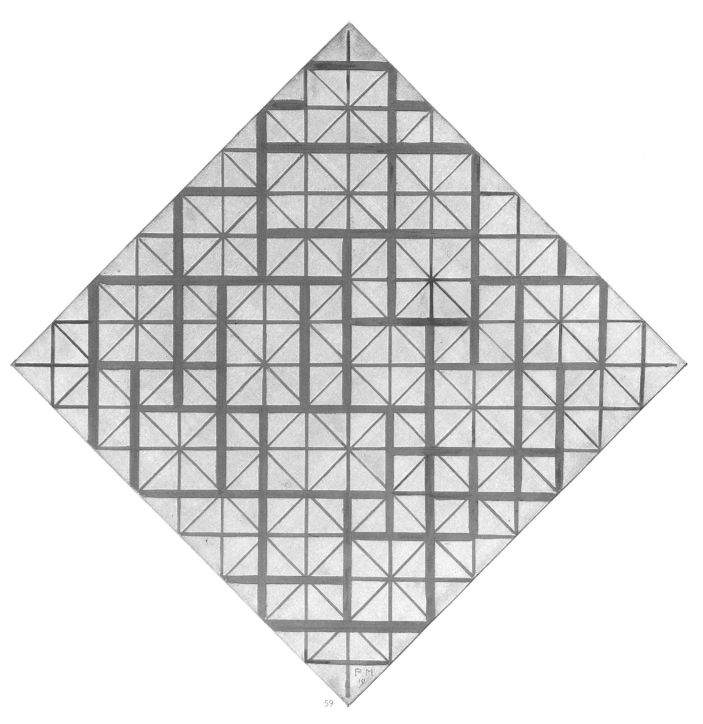

59

59
*Composition in Black and
Grey,* 1919
Oil on canvas,
$23^3/_4 \times 23^1/_2$ in.
(60.3 × 59.7 cm)
Philadelphia Museum of Art,
Louise and Walter
Arensberg Collection

60

60
*Composition: Bright Colours
with Grey Lines*, 1919
Oil on canvas,
19 1/4 × 19 1/4 in. (49 × 49 cm)
Oeffentliche Kunstammlung,
Kunstmuseum, Basel
Gift of Marguerite
Arp-Hagenbach, 1968
Photograph: Martin Bohler

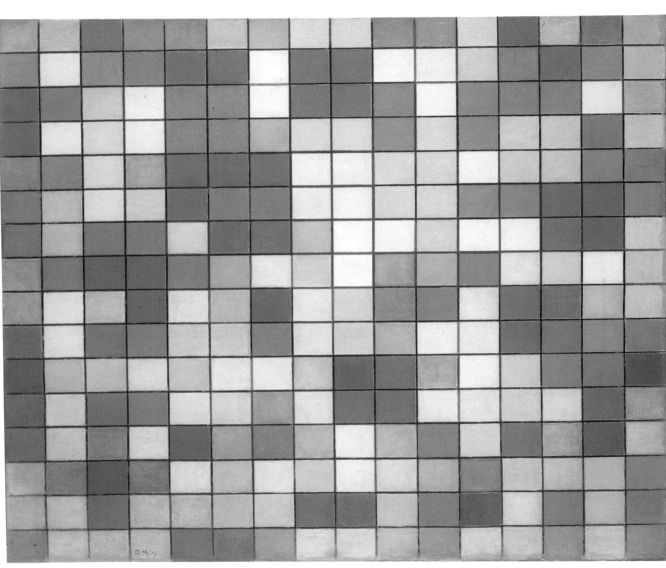

61

61
*Composition: Checkerboard.
Light Colours*, 1919
Oil on canvas,
33 7/8 × 41 3/4 in. (86 × 106 cm)
Gemeentemuseum,
The Hague

62

62
Composition with Red, Blue and Yellow-Green, 1920
Oil on canvas,
26³/₈×22¹/₂ in. (67×57 cm)
Wilhelm Hack Museum,
Ludwigshafen

63
Composition with Red, Yellow and Blue, 1920
Oil on canvas,
20¹/₄×24 in. (51.5×61 cm)
Stedelijk Museum,
Amsterdam

63

64

64
Large Composition A, 1920
Oil on canvas,
35 $^1/_2$ × 35 $^3/_4$ in.
(90.2 × 90.8 cm)
Galleria Nazionale d'Arte
Moderna, Rome

65
Composition with Grey, Red,
Yellow and Blue, 1920–1926
Oil on canvas,
39 1/4×39 1/2 in.
(99.6×100.3 cm)
Tate Gallery, London

66
Composition with Red, Yellow
and Blue, 1921
Oil on canvas,
31 1/2×19 3/4 in. (80×50 cm)
Gemeentemuseum,
The Hague

68

67
Tableau I, 1921
Oil on canvas,
37 3/4 × 23 5/8 in. (96×60 cm)
Museum Ludwig, Cologne
Photograph: Rheinisches
Bildarchiv, Cologne

68
*Composition with Red, Yellow
and Blue*, 1921
Oil on canvas,
40 1/2 × 39 3/8 in. (103×100 cm)
Gemeentemuseum,
The Hague

69

69
*Composition with Large Blue
Plane*, 1921
Oil on canvas,
23³/₄ × 19³/₄ in. (60.5 × 50 cm)
Dallas Museum of Art,
Foundation for the Arts
Collection
Gift of Mrs James H Clark

70
*Composition with Red, Yellow
and Blue*, 1922
Oil on canvas,
16¹/₂ × 19³/₄ in. (42 × 50 cm)
Stedelijk Museum,
Amsterdam

70

71

72

71
Painting No. 11, 1922
Oil on canvas,
15¹/₈×13⁵/₈ in.
(38.5×34.5 cm)
Kaiser Wilhelm Museum,
Krefeld

72
*Composition with Red, Yellow
and Blue*, 1922
Oil on canvas,
16¹/₂×19¹/₄ in.
(41.9×48.9 cm)
The Minneapolis Institute
of Arts

73
Composition I with Blue and
Yellow, 1925
Oil on canvas,
44 1/8 × 44 1/8 in. (112 × 112 cm)
Kunsthaus, Zurich
Association des Amis
Zurichois de l'art

74

74
*Diamond Painting in Red,
Yellow and Blue*, 1921–1925
Oil on canvas,
56 1/4 × 56 in.
(142.8 × 142.3 cm)
National Gallery of Art,
Washington
Gift of Herbert and
Nannette Rothschild

75

75
Painting II (Composition in Grey and Black), 1925
Oil on canvas,
19³/₄ × 19³/₄ in. (50 × 50 cm)
Kunstmuseum, Berne Max
Huggler-Stiftung

76
*Composition with Blue, Grey,
Red, White*, 1926
Oil on canvas,
15³/₄ × 11⁷/₈ in. (40 × 30 cm)
Kaiser Wilhelm Museum,
Krefeld

77
*Composition with Red, Yellow
and Blue*, 1927
Oil on canvas,
24 × 15³/₄ in. (61 × 40 cm)
Stedelijk Museum,
Amsterdam

76

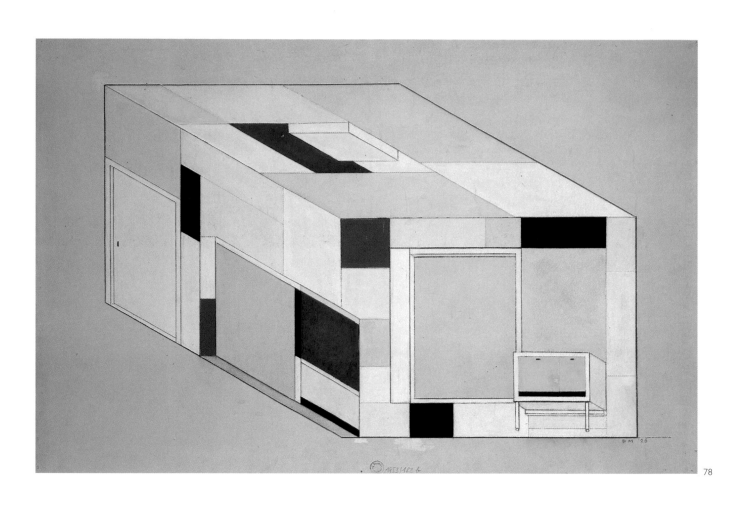

80

81

82

78
Salon de Mme B à Dresde,
Exploded box plan, 1926
Ink and gouache,
27³/₄×27³/₄ in.
(70.5×70.5 cm)
Staatliche Kunstsammlungen,
Dresden

79
Salon de Mme B. à Dresde,
perspective drawing, 1926
Ink and gouache,
14³/₄×22¹/₂ in. (37.5×57 cm)
Staatliche Kunstsammlungen,
Dresden

80–82
Maquette of set for M.
Seuphor, *L'Ephémère est*
éternel', 1926
(Reconstruction by Ad
Dekkers, 1964)
Wood and card,
21×30¹/₈×10¹/₂ in.
(53.3×76.5×26.5 cm)
Van Abbemuseum,
Eindhoven

83

83
Composition with Red, Yellow and Blue, 1927
Oil on canvas,
20 1/8 × 20 1/8 in. (51 × 51 cm)
Cleveland Museum of Art

84
Composition with Red, Yellow and Blue, 1928
Oil on canvas,
17 3/4 × 17 3/4 in. (45 × 45 cm)
Wilhelm Hack Museum,
Ludwigshaven

84

85

86

85
Composition, 1929
Oil on canvas,
$20^5/8 \times 20^5/8$ in.
(52.5×52.5 cm)
Oeffentliche Kunstammlung,
Kunstmusuem, Basel
Gift of Marguerite Arp-
Hagenbach, 1968
Photograph: Martin Bohler

86
*Composition with Yellow and
Blue*, 1929
Oil on canvas,
$20^1/2 \times 20^1/2$ in. (52×52 cm)
Museum Boymans van
Beuningen, Rotterdam

87

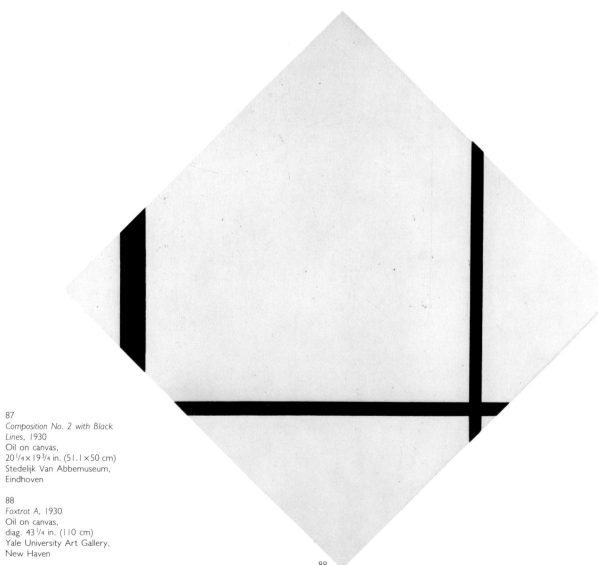

87
*Composition No. 2 with Black
Lines*, 1930
Oil on canvas,
20 1/4 × 19 3/4 in. (51.1×50 cm)
Stedelijk Van Abbemuseum,
Eindhoven

88
Foxtrot A, 1930
Oil on canvas,
diag. 43 1/4 in. (110 cm)
Yale University Art Gallery,
New Haven

88

89

89
Composition with Red, Yellow and Blue, 1935
Oil on canvas,
21 $^{5}/_{8}$ × 21 $^{5}/_{8}$ in. (55 × 55 cm)
Tate Gallery, London

90

90
Composition with Two Lines,
1931
Oil on canvas,
diag. 44⁷/8 in. (114 cm)
Stedelijk Museum,
Amsterdam

91

91
Composition with Yellow Lines,
1933
Oil on canvas,
diag 44$^1/_2$ in. (113 cm)
Gemeentemuseum,
The Hague

92
Grey-Red Composition, 1935
Oil on canvas,
23 5/8 × 22 3/8 in. (60×56.8 cm)
The Art Institute of Chicago
Gift of Mrs Gilbert W
Chapman
Photograph by permission of
Art Institute of Chicago

93
*Composition with Blue, Yellow
and White*, 1936
Oil on canvas,
17 1/8 × 13 1/4 in.
(43.5×33.5 cm)
Emmanuel Hoffmann
Foundation, Basel
Photograph: Martin Bohler

94

94
Composition with Red and Blue, 1936
Oil on canvas,
38⁵/₈×31⁵/₈ in (98×80.3 cm)
Staatsgalerie, Stuttgart

95
*Vertical Composition with Blue
and White*, 1936
Oil on canvas,
47 $^{5}/_{8}$ × 23 $^{1}/_{4}$ in. (121 × 59 cm)
Kunstsammlung Nordrhein-
Westfalen, Dusseldorf

95

96

97

96
Composition with Red, Yellow and Blue, 1936–1943
Oil on canvas,
23 1/4 × 21 1/4 in. (59 × 54 cm)
Moderna Museet, Stockholm

97
Composition 12 with Small Blue Square, 1936–1943
Oil on canvas,
24 3/4 × 23 7/8 in. (62 × 60.5 cm)
The National Gallery of Canada, Ottawa

98

98
Composition with White,
Black and Red, 1936
Oil on canvas,
40 1/8 × 41 in. (102×104 cm)
Collection of The Museum
of Modern Art, New York
Donation Advisory
Committee
Photograph © (1933) The
Museum of Modern Art,
New York

99

99
*Composition with Red, Yellow
and Blue,* 1939–1942
Oil on canvas,
28 5/8 × 27 1/4 in.
(72.7 × 69.2 cm)
Tate Gallery, London

100

100
*Composition with Red and
Yellow*, 1937
Oil on canvas,
17×13 in. (43.3×33 cm)
Philadelphia Museum of Art:
The A.E. Gallatin Collection

101

101
Composition 2, 1937
Oil on canvas,
29 1/2 × 23 7/8 in. (75 × 60.5 cm)
Musée National d'Art
Moderne, Centre Georges
Pompidou, Paris

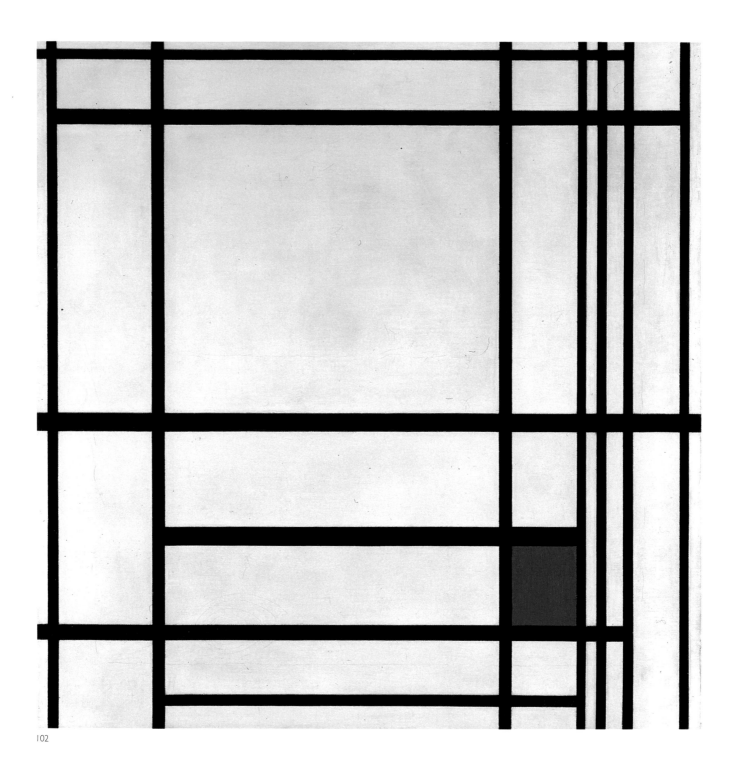

102

103

103
Composition with Red and White, 1938–1942
Oil on canvas,
39 1/2 × 39 in. (100.3 × 99.1 cm)
The Saint Louis Art Museum
Acquisition: Friends' Fund

104

104
Composition with Red, 1939
Oil on canvas,
41 $^1/_2$ × 40 $^1/_4$ in.
(105.2 × 102.3 cm)
Collection Peggy
Guggenheim, Venice
Photograph: David Heald,
© (1991) The Solomon
R. Guggenheim Foundation

105

106

107

107
Place de la Concorde
1939–1943
Oil on canvas,
37×37⁵/₈ in. (94×95.5 cm)
Dallas Museum of Art,
Foundation for the Arts
Collection
Gift of James H and Lillian
Clark Foundation

108

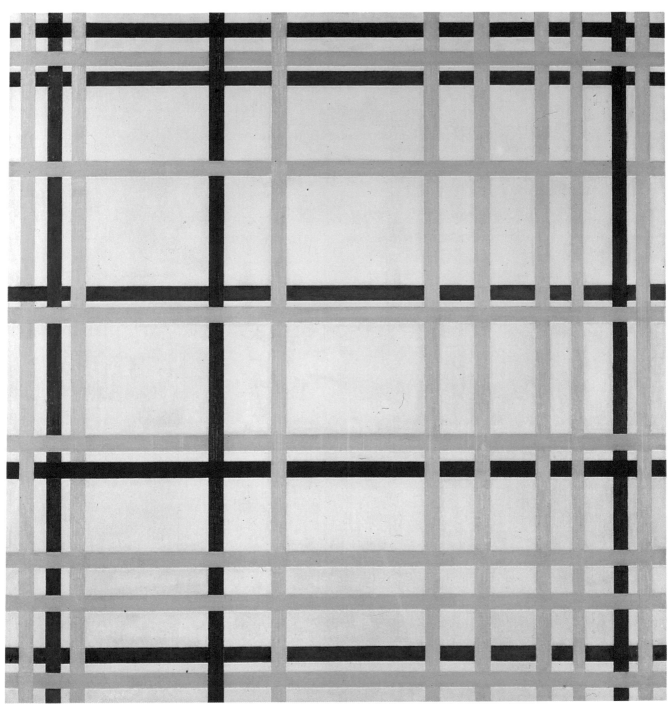

109

109
New York City I, 1942
Oil on canvas,
47 1/4×45 in. (120×114.3 cm)
Musée National d'Art
Moderne, Centre Georges
Pompidou, Paris

110

110
New York City II, 1942–1944
Oil and paper tape on canvas,
47×45 in. (119.4×114.3 cm)
Kunstammlung Nordrhein-
Westfalen, Dusseldorf

111

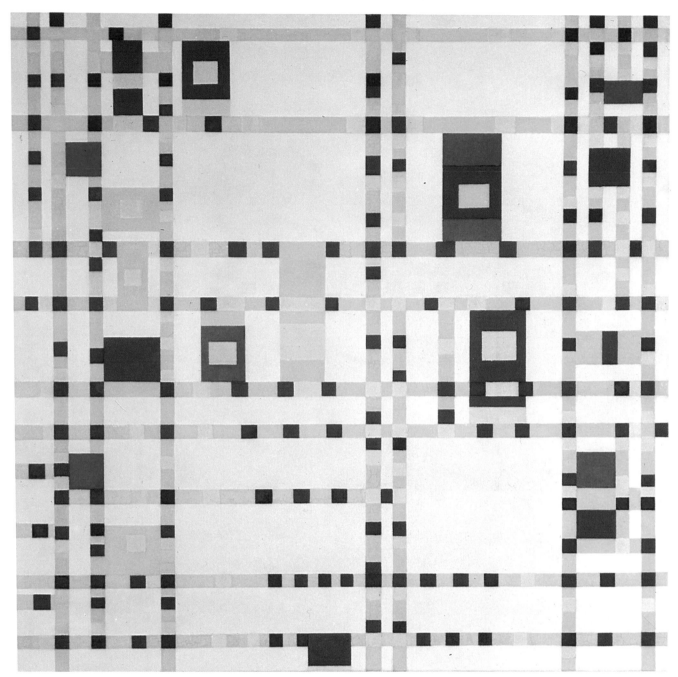

111
Broadway Boogie-Woogie,
1942–1943
Oil on canvas,
50×50 in. (127×127 cm)
Collection of The Museum
of Modern Art, New York
Anonymous gift
Photograph © (1993) The
Museum of Modern Art,
New York

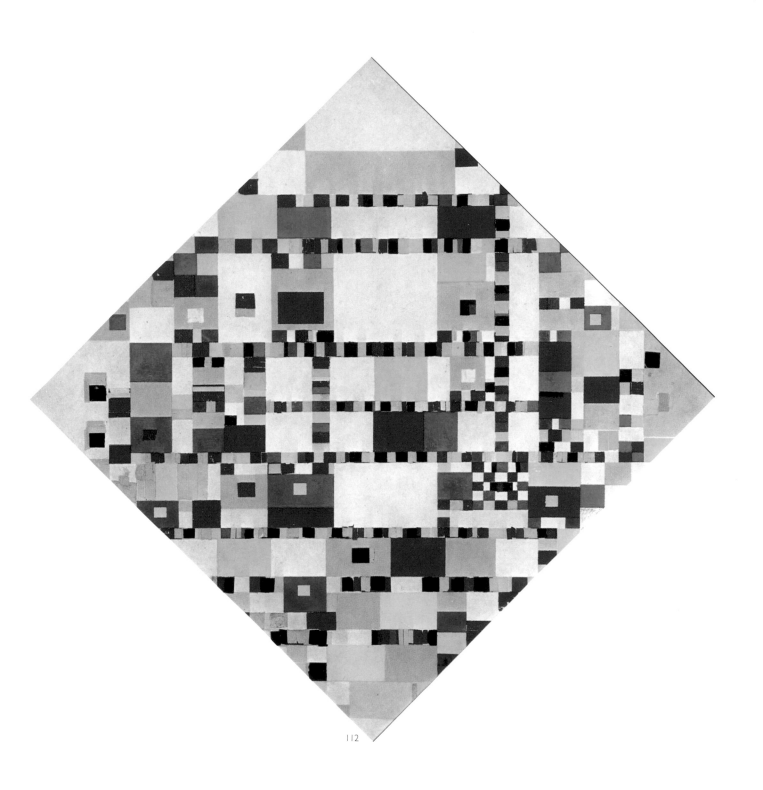

112

112
Victory Boogie-Woogie,
1943–1944 (Unfinished)
Oil on canvas with coloured
tape and paper,
diag. 70 1/4 in. (178.5 cm)
Burton Tremaine Collection,
Meriden, Connecticut

LIST OF ILLUSTRATIONS

21
Wood near Oele, 1908
Oil on canvas,
11×62 1/4 in. (28×158 cm)
Gemeentemuseum, The Hague

22
Rhododendrons, 1909–1910
Charcoal and pastel on beige paper,
28 3/4×38 3/8 in. (73×97.5 cm)
Gemeentemuseum, The Hague

23
Sunflower II, 1907–1908
Oil on card,
25 5/8×13 3/8 in. (65×34 cm)
Gemeentemuseum, The Hague

24
Chrysanthemum, 1909
Gouache,
27 1/8×10 3/4 in. (69×26.5 cm)
Gemeentemuseum, The Hague

25
The Tree, c. 1908
Oil on canvas,
42 7/8×28 1/2 in. (109.2×72.4 cm)
McNay Art Museum, San Antonio,
Texas Gift of Alice Hanszen

26
Dune II, 1909–1910
Oil on canvas,
15×18 1/4 in. (38×46.5 cm)
Gemeentemuseum, The Hague

27
Dune IV, 1909–1910
Oil on canvas,
13×18 1/8 in. (33×46 cm)
Gemeentemuseum, The Hague

28
Zeeland Farmer, 1909–1910
Oil on canvas,
27 1/8×20 7/8 in. (69×53 cm)
Gemeentemuseum, The Hague

29
Lighthouse near Westkapelle,
1909–1910
Oil on canvas,
53 1/8×29 1/2 in. (135×75 cm)
Gemeentemuseum, The Hague

30
Lighthouse near Westkapelle,
1908–1909
Ink, pencil and gouache,
11 7/8×9 5/8 in. (30×24.5 cm)
Gemeentemuseum, The Hague

31
Passion Flower, 1908–1909
Watercolour,
28 1/2×18 1/4 in. (72.5×46.5 cm)
Gemeentemuseum, The Hague

32
Nude, 1908–1911
Black chalk,
33 7/8×16 1/2 in. (86×42 cm)
Gemeentemuseum, The Hague

33
Evolution, 1910–1911
Oil on canvas, triptych,
70 1/8×33 1/2 in., 72×34 1/2 1/2 in.,
70 1/2×33 1/2 in. (178×85 cm,
183×87.5 cm, 178×85 cm)
Gemeentemuseum, The Hague

34
Church in Domburg, 1910–1911
Oil on canvas,
44 7/8×29 1/2 in. (114×75 cm)
Gemeentemuseum, The Hague

35
Landscape: Dunes, c 1911
Oil on canvas,
55 1/2×94 1/8 in. (141×239 cm)
Gemeentemuseum, The Hague

36
The Red Mill, 1911
Oil on canvas,
59×33 7/8 in. (150×86 cm)
Gemeentemuseum, The Hague

37
Still Life with Ginger Pot I, 1911–1912
Oil on canvas,
25 3/4×29 1/2 in. (65.5×75 cm)
Gemeentemuseum, The Hague

38
Nude, 1912
Oil on canvas,
55 1/8×38 5/8 in. (140×98 cm)
Gemeentemuseum, The Hague

39
Still Life with Ginger Pot II, 1912
Oil on canvas,
36×47 1/4 in. (91.5×120 cm)
Gemeentemuseum, The Hague

40
Landscape with Trees, 1912
Oil on canvas,
47 1/4×39 3/8 in. (120×100 cm)
Gemeentemuseum, The Hague

41
Tree, c. 1912
Oil on canvas,
37×27 7/8 in. (94×70.8 cm)
Carnegie Institute, Museum of Art,
Pittsburgh

42
Apple Tree in Blossom, 1912
Oil on canvas,
30 3/4×41 3/4 in. (78×106 cm)
Gemeentemuseum, The Hague

43
Composition: Trees II, 1912–1913
Oil on canvas,
38 5/8×25 5/8 in. (98×65 cm)
Gemeentemuseum, The Hague

44
Composition of Lines and Colours,
1913
Oil on canvas,
25 1/4×37 in. (64.1×94 cm)
Rijksmuseum Kröller-Müller, Otterlo

45
Composition VII, 1913
Oil on canvas,
41 1/8×44 3/4 in. (104.4×113.6 cm)
The Solomon R. Guggenheim
Foundation, New York
Photograph: David Heald,
© The Solomon R. Guggenheim
Foundation, New York

46
*Composition of Lines and Colours
(Windmill)*, 1913
Oil on canvas,
45 1/4×34 5/8 in. (115×88 cm)
Rijksmuseum Kröller-Müller, Otterlo

47
Oval Composition III, 1914
Oil on canvas,
55 1/8×39 3/4 in. (140×101 cm)
Stedelijk Museum, Amsterdam

48
Oval Composition (Trees), 1913
Oil on canvas,
37×29 7/8 in. (94×76 cm)
Stedelijk Musuem, Amsterdam

49
Colour Planes in an Oval,
1913–1914
Oil on canvas,
42 3/8×31 in. (107.6×78.8 cm)
Collection of the Museum of Modern
Art, New York (Acquisition)
Photograph © (1993) The Museum
of Modern Art, New York

50
Composition in an Oval: KUB,
1914
Oil on canvas,
44 1/2×33 1/4 in. (113×81.5 cm)
Gemeentemuseum, The Hague

51
Farm at Duivendrecht,
1915–1916
(or 1906–1908)
Oil on canvas,
33 5/8×42 3/4 in. (85.5×108.5 cm)
Gemeentemuseum, The Hague

52
Composition No. 10, 1915
Oil on canvas,
33 1/2×42 1/2 in. (85×108 cm)
Rijksmuseum Kröller-Müller, Otterlo

53
Self-Portrait, 1918
Oil on canvas,
34 5/8×28 in. (88×71 cm)
Gemeentemuseum, The Hague

54
Composition with Colour Planes A,
1917
Oil on canvas,
19 3/4×17 3/8 in. (50×44 cm)
Rijksmuseum Kröller-Müller, Otterlo

55
Composition with Colour Planes No. 3,
1917
Oil on canvas,
18 7/8×24 in. (48×61 cm)
Gemeentemuseum, The Hague

56
Composition in Black and White, 1917
Oil on canvas,
42 1/5×42 1/2 in. (108×108 cm)
Rijksmuseum Kröller-Müller, Otterlo

57
Composition, 1916
Oil on canvas,
46 7/8×29 1/2 in. (119×75.1 cm)
The Solomon R. Guggenheim
Foundation, New York
Photograph: David Heald,
© The Solomon R. Guggenheim
Foundation, New York

58
Composition in Diamond Shape,
1918–1919
Oil on canvas, 26 1/4 in. (67 cm)
Rijksemusem Kröller-Müller, Otterlo

59
Composition in Black and Grey, 1919
Oil on canvas,
23 3/4×23 1/2 in. (60.3×59.7 cm)
Philadelphia Museum of Art, Louise
and Walter Arensberg Collection

60
*Composition: Bright Colours with Grey
Lines*, 1919
Oil on canvas,
19 1/4×19 1/4 in. (49×49 cm)
Oeffentliche Kunstammlung,
Kunstmuseum, Basel
Gift of Marguerite Arp-Hagenbach,
1968
Photograph: Martin Bohler

61
*Composition: Checkerboard, Light
Colours*, 1919
Oil on canvas,
33 7/8×41 3/4 in. (86×106 cm)
Gemeentemuseum, The Hague

62
*Composition with Red, Blue and
Yellow-Green*, 1920
Oil on canvas,
26 3/8×22 1/2 in. (67×57 cm)
Wilhelm Hack Museum, Ludwigshafen

63
*Composition with Red, Yellow and
Blue*, 1920
Oil on canvas,
20 1/4×24 in. (51.5×61 cm)
Stedelijk Museum, Amsterdam

64
Large Composition A, 1920
Oil on canvas,
35 1/2×35 3/4 in. (90.2×90.8 cm)
Galleria Nazionale d'Arte Moderna,
Rome

65
*Composition with Grey, Red, Yellow
and Blue*, 1920–1926
Oil on canvas,
39 1/4×39 1/2 in. (99.6×100.3 cm)
Tate Gallery, London

66
*Composition with Red, Yellow and
Blue*, 1921
Oil on canvas,
31 1/2×19 3/4 in. (80×50 cm)
Gemeentemuseum, The Hague

67
Tableau I, 1921
Oil on canvas,
37 3/4×23 5/8 in. (96×60 cm)
Museum Ludwig, Cologne
Photograph: Rheinisches Bildarchiv,
Cologne

68
*Composition with Red, Yellow and
Blue*, 1921
Oil on canvas,
40 1/2×39 3/8 in. (103×100 cm)
Gemeentemuseum, The Hague

69
Composition with Large Blue Plane,
1921
Oil on canvas,
23 3/4×19 3/4 in. (60.5×50 cm)
Dallas Museum of Art, Foundation
for the Arts Collection
Gift of Mrs James H Clark

70
*Composition with Red, Yellow and
Blue*, 1922
Oil on canvas,
16 1/2×19 3/4 in. (42×50 cm)
Stedelijk Museum, Amsterdam

71
Painting No. 11, 1922
Oil on canvas,
15 1/8 × 13 5/8 in. (38.5 × 34.5 cm)
Kaiser Wilhelm Museum, Krefeld

72
Composition with Red, Yellow and Blue, 1922
Oil on canvas,
16 1/2 × 19 1/4 in. (41.9 × 48.9 cm)
The Minneapolis Institute of Arts

73
Composition I with Blue and Yellow, 1925
Oil on canvas,
44 1/8 × 44 1/8 in. (112 × 112 cm)
Kunsthaus, Zurich Association des Amis Zurichois de l'art

74
Diamond Painting in Red, Yellow and Blue, 1921–1925
Oil on canvas,
56 1/4 × 56 in. (142.8 × 142.3 cm)
National Gallery of Art, Washington
Gift of Herbert and Nannette Rothschild

75
Painting II (Composition in Grey and Black), 1925
Oil on canvas,
19 3/4 × 19 3/4 in. (50 × 50 cm)
Kunstmuseum, Berne Max Huggler-Stiftung

76
Composition with Blue, Grey, Red, White, 1926
Oil on canvas,
15 3/4 × 11 7/8 in. (40 × 30 cm)
Kaiser Wilhelm Museum, Krefeld

77
Composition with Red, Yellow and Blue, 1927
Oil on canvas,
24 × 15 3/4 in. (61 × 40 cm)
Stedelijk Museum, Amsterdam

78
Salon de Mme B à Dresde, Exploded box plan, 1926
Ink and gouache,
27 3/4 × 27 3/4 in. (70.5 × 70.5 cm)
Staatliche Kunstsammlungen, Dresden

79
Salon de Mme B. à Dresde, perspective drawing, 1926
Ink and gouache,
14 3/4 × 22 1/2 in. (37.5 × 57 cm)
Staatliche Kunstsammlungen, Dresden

80–82
Maquette of set for M. Seuphor, *L'Ephémère est éternel'*, 1926
(Reconstruction by Ad Dekkers, 1964)
Wood and card, 21 × 30 1/8 × 10 1/2 in. (53.3 × 76.5 × 26.5 cm)
Van Abbemuseum, Eindhoven

83
Composition with Red, Yellow and Blue, 1927
Oil on canvas,
20 1/8 × 20 1/8 in. (51 × 51 cm)
Cleveland Museum of Art

84
Composition with Red, Yellow and Blue, 1928
Oil on canvas,
17 3/4 × 17 3/4 in. (45 × 45 cm)
Wilhelm Hack Museum, Ludwigshaven

85
Composition, 1929
Oil on canvas,
20 5/8 × 20 5/8 in. (52.5 × 52.5 cm)
Oeffentliche Kunstammlung, Kunstmuseum, Basel
Gift of Marguerite Arp-Hagenbach, 1968
Photograph: Martin Bohler

86
Composition with Yellow and Blue, 1929
Oil on canvas,
20 1/2 × 20 1/2 in. (52 × 52 cm)
Museum Boymans van Beuningen, Rotterdam

87
Composition No. 2 with Black Lines, 1930
Oil on canvas,
20 1/4 × 19 3/4 in. (51.1 × 50 cm)
Stedelijk Van Abbemuseum, Eindhoven

88
Foxtrot A, 1930
Oil on canvas, diag. 43 1/4 in. (110 cm)
Yale University Art Gallery, New Haven

89
Composition with Red, Yellow and Blue, 1935
Oil on canvas,
21 5/8 × 21 5/8 in. (55 × 55 cm)
Tate Gallery, London

90
Composition with Two Lines, 1931
Oil on canvas, diag. 44 7/8 in. (114 cm)
Stedelijk Museum, Amsterdam

91
Composition with Yellow Lines, 1933
Oil on canvas, diag 44 1/2 in. (113 cm)
Gemeentemuseum, The Hague

92
Grey-Red Composition, 1935
Oil on canvas,
23 5/8 × 22 3/8 in. (60 × 56.8 cm)
The Art Institute of Chicago
Gift of Mrs Gilbert W Chapman
Photograph by permission of Art Institute of Chicago

93
Composition with Blue, Yellow and White, 1936
Oil on canvas,
17 1/8 × 13 1/4 in. (43.5 × 33.5 cm)
Emmanuel Hoffmann Foundation, Basel
Photograph: Martin Bohler

94
Composition with Red and Blue, 1936
Oil on canvas,
38 5/8 × 31 5/8 in (98 × 80.3 cm)
Staatsgalerie, Stuttgart

95
Vertical Composition with Blue and White, 1936
Oil on canvas,
47 5/8 × 23 1/4 in. (121 × 59 cm)
Kunstsammlung Nordrhein-Westfalen, Dusseldorf

96
Composition with Red, Yellow and Blue, 1936–1943
Oil on canvas,
23 1/4 × 21 1/4 in. (59 × 54 cm)
Moderna Museet, Stockholm

97
Composition 12 with Small Blue Square, 1936–1943
Oil on canvas,
24 3/4 × 23 7/8 in. (62 × 60.5 cm)
The National Gallery of Canada, Ottawa

98
Composition with White, Black and Red, 1936
Oil on canvas,
40 1/8 × 41 in. (102 × 104 cm)
Collection of The Museum of Modern Art, New York
Donation Advisory Committee
Photograph © (1933) The Museum of Modern Art, New York

99
Composition with Red, Yellow and Blue, 1939–1942
Oil on canvas,
28 5/8 × 27 1/4 in. (72.7 × 69.2 cm)
Tate Gallery, London

100
Composition with Red and Yellow, 1937
Oil on canvas, 17 × 13 in. (43.3 × 33 cm)
Philadelphia Museum of Art:
The A.E. Gallatin Collection

101
Composition 2, 1937
Oil on canvas,
29 1/2 × 23 7/8 in. (75 × 60.5 cm)
Musée National d'Art Moderne, Centre Georges Pompidou, Paris

102
Composition with Blue, 1937
Oil on canvas,
31 1/2 × 30 3/8 in. (80 × 77 cm)
Gemeentemuseum, The Hague

103
Composition with Red and White, 1938–1942
Oil on canvas,
39 1/2 × 39 in. (100.3 × 99.1 cm)
The Saint Louis Art Museum
Acquisition: Friends' Fund

104
Composition with Red, 1939
Oil on canvas,
41 1/2 × 40 1/4 in. (105.2 × 102.3 cm)
Collection Peggy Guggenheim, Venice
Photograph: David Heald, © (1991)
The Solomon R. Guggenheim Foundation

105
Painting No. 9, 1939–1942
Oil on canvas,
31 1/4 × 29 1/8 in. (79.4 × 74 cm)
The Phillips Collection, Washington DC

106
Composition: London, 1940–1942
Oil on canvas,
32 1/2 × 28 in. (82.5 × 71 cm)
Albright-Knox Gallery, Buffalo, New York
Room of Contemporary Art Fund

107
Place de la Concorde, 1939–1943
Oil on canvas,
37 × 37 5/8 in. (94 × 95.5 cm)
Dallas Museum of Art, Foundation for the Arts Collection
Gift of James H and Lillian Clark Foundation

108
Trafalgar Square, 1939–1943
Oil on canvas,
57 1/8 × 47 1/4 in. (145 × 120 cm)
Collection of The Museum of Modern Art, New York
Gift of Mr. and Mrs. William A.M. Burden
Photograph © (1993) The Museum of Modern Art, New York

109
New York City I, 1942
Oil on canvas,
47 1/4 × 45 in. (120 × 114.3 cm)
Musée National d'Art Moderne, Centre Georges Pompidou, Paris

110
New York City II, 1942–1944
Oil and paper tape on canvas,
47 × 45 in. (119.4 × 114.3 cm)
Kunstammlung Nordrhein-Westfalen, Dusseldorf

111
Broadway Boogie-Woogie, 1942–1943
Oil on canvas, 50 × 50 in. (127 × 127 cm)
Collection of The Museum of Modern Art, New York
Anonymous gift
Photograph © (1993) The Museum of Modern Art, New York

112
Victory Boogie-Woogie, 1943–1944
(Unfinished)
Oil on canvas with coloured tape and paper, diag. 70 1/4 in. (1785 cm)
Burton Tremaine Collection, Meriden, Connecticut